D1282571

BY TADEUSZ KONWICKI

A Dreambook for Our Time
Anthropos-Specter-Beast
The Polish Complex
A Minor Apocalypse
Moonrise, Moonset
Bohin Manor
New World Avenue
and Vicinity

NEW WORLD AVENUE
and Vicinity

NEW WORLD AVENUE
and Vicinity

TADEUSZ KONWICKI

Translated by Walter Arndt

with Drawings by the Author

Farrar, Straus and Giroux

New York

Library of Congress Cataloging-in-Publication Data
Konwicki, Tadeusz.
[Nowy Świat i okolice. English]
New World Avenue and Vicinity / Tadeusz Konwicki ; translated by
Walter Arndt ; with drawings by the author. — 1st ed.
p. cm.
Translation of: Nowy Świat i okolice.
I. Title
PG7158.K6513N4813 1991   891.8'537—dc20   90-48492

NEW WORLD AVENUE
and Vicinity

labyrinth

New World Avenue

It is with a heavy heart that I get down to writing yet another book that nobody needs. At this point, of course, one or the other charitable reader will protest and assure me that I am wrong, that my books fill a need with juveniles, adults, even those decrepit with age. I am aware, though, that from time to time someone will reach for something I have written, browse in it for a while, inspect it from one side and another, and eventually put it aside among other unfinished, unappreciated, uncherished books. I know all about myself and all about my colleagues, rivals, competitors. I know all about my kind and not so kind readers. I know enough to make me never reach for a pen again.

But, after all, I did fill the old pen with some of the old ink, which for reasons unknown turned up in the lumber the other day. I wait for the night, for that sonorous silence of the Warsaw tenement just before midnight, and behind the back of wife and children I begin to run the old pen over old paper (my paper is old, too). And in order to make the outlandish undertaking, that shocking project of an old backslider, more difficult for myself; to complicate, that is to say, the writing of that book nobody needs, not myself, not my poor family or my down-trodden fellow countrymen; to punish myself, you see, for these salacious appetites, I resolve to write a book for the regular state publishing house, a book which I propose to censor myself, carefully and expertly. Our paths have parted long since, mine and that of the censorship office. Time was when it was my first penetrating reader, my confidant, my inimical friend or friendly enemy. Later, though, we lost sight of each other, and I became unaccustomed to my first penetrating reader, unknown confidant, and hostile friend. Uncontrolled, deprived of tender care, lost to ideological canon and civic gravity, I wrote whatever spittle washed to tongue, spavined novels and misbegotten memoirs.

Now it is back to the yoke with me. Of my own free will I submit to the loving embrace of the noble agency which presides on Mysia Street in Warsaw. And from this moment I am safe. Henceforth the course of my pen is tracked by the vigilant eye of my unknown guardian, my intellectual father, my spiritual guide. What a safe and blissful feeling it is. At last.

So, for the first time in my life, I am writing a book for the censors. I have grown disillusioned with readers, offended by their inattention, disenchanted by their superficial reaction, turned off by their ruthless betrayals. How many times has it happened to me that some new acquaintance has gone into raptures, tenderly squeezed my hands, and assured me that he knew my books by heart. I, tickled pink in the vanity gland, would spread my tail feathers behind the table, show off, pontificate, until by some unhappy chance I would refer to my Wilno parentage. At which point my admirer would generally raise his eyebrows and say: "Oh? You're from Wilno? My aunt was born in Wilno, too!"

Here I should explain to my admirers that all my books are stuffed full of Wilno, that I go round and round forever writing about Wilno, that actually I have been writing one and the same book all my life, a novel of identical content each time, identical plot, identical characters. I didn't even exert myself on descriptions of nature; I have been shoveling out the same old thing for twenty years.

I can afford such easements of the novelistic toil because I noticed a long time ago that the contemporary reader has the memory of a chicken. He is incapable of remembering either a thought or a protagonist, or even the author. It does happen that a brighter specimen of reader has memorized some witticism from my book and springs it on me over a drink as his own. But I am not slow to repay him; I have no compunction about serving the fellow some quotation from that book of mine which he has just laid aside. And he will go all goggle-eyed over this novelty and be happy.

So this is why I have been writing the same book over and over again for twenty years. And behind it is not some sort of high-flown consistency or noble unity of subject matter or any exalted creative obsession. No—all it is is a convenience my reader has got me used to.

But at this point, be it out of some frivolous or clowning mood or out of ultimate despair, I choose for a friend, right to the last page, the anonymous censor, who for a modest salary will accompany me on a wondrous voyage full of geographical curiosities, who will tenderly guide my aging hand with its aging Waterman pen, who will rule out unnecessary words and equivocal thoughts and illuminate my old sinful head with right thinking.

But let us return to New World Avenue.

New World Avenue, Once Again

New World is the name of a street in Warsaw. Every old city has a New World. There came a time when it got too tight in the towns that were choked by defensive bastions, and one fine day, life swept over those walls, and across the moats, and into the free spaces of meadows, coppices, and brooks. This is how new worlds arose. Including the new world beyond the ocean.

In my native Wilno the new world was known, adopting the

Belorussian, as *nowostrojka*, "new construction" or "outbor-
oughs." But I have never been there, I know that bandits'
quarter only from bedtime tales or yarns repeated by schoolboys
who puffed stolen cigarettes near the school fence.

Warsaw's New World I saw for the first time in 1947, when
I moved there from Cracow, along with the weekly magazine
Rebirth, of which I was technical manager at the time, or perhaps
already editorial secretary. The man who transferred us was
Jerzy Borejsza, president of the Czytelnik publishing house,
which at that time was a preternaturally gigantic concern, perhaps even bigger than the largest American ones, an unexam-
pled prodigy of human imagination, resourcefulness, and
goodwill in a country that was totally devastated and reluctantly
accepting a new faith from the East.

So Borejsza moved us to Warsaw, prompted by a whim worthy of Hearst, and established us in the Bristol, the famous
Warsaw hotel, which by a strange quirk of fate had survived
amid an ocean of rubble. And I, twenty years old, still a clodhopper, a greenhorn with the eggshells of Wilno still on me,
took up residence in an elegant apartment next door to dip-
lomats, ministers of state, generals. I was able to lounge on
those Bristol sofas perhaps six months before, by another stroke
of magic, President Borejsza moved me to Frascati Street and
thoughtfully set me down in a sunny little room with a small
kitchen, fit for a cabinet member or a speculator.

My point here is that between the Bristol and Frascati Street
runs New World Avenue, that storied tract of Polish kings,
which in those years was a narrow footpath in a canyon of ruins,
sparsely grown over with dry grass and frail little birches. By
that footpath, tortuous and full of holes, I used to walk from
the Bristol to the print shop on Union of Lublin Square; and
later, after my move to Frascati Street, the same royal ravine
took me of a Sunday for walks in the direction of the Old Town.
I should mention that these were hazardous expeditions: past
the Bristol, which was the last outpost of civilization, you found
yourself in a wilderness reminiscent of the Rocky Mountains,
where you were apt to lose your watch, your wallet, quite possibly your life.

The muggers of Warsaw had a certain polish in those days. Any roughness or vulgarity was absolutely out. The Warsaw bandit would lean out of the darkness and politely suggest a business transaction: Want to buy a brick? And all about, the neighborhood ladies of easy virtue wafted like specters. They were punningly called *Gruzinki*, "Georgian girls," because they plied their trade in the ruins (*gruzy*).

Later, it is hard to tell exactly when, New World Avenue rose from the ruins. Abruptly, in the course of two or three years, it became a reputable street modeled on the paintings of the nephew of Canaletto. Very quickly life took root in those ersatz historic eighteenth-century landmarks—a poorer and grayer life, granted, but making up for it in aggressiveness, greed, and the habit of success. I, too, turned up there as a lodger in a new apartment house on Górski Street, which branches off from Szpitalna Street, with its rear abutting on the gate of 41 New World Avenue.

This New World Avenue is my track to a luminous future, or my Golgotha marked by the Stations of my Passion, yet to be detailed by me at the proper time. This is the street, curved like a Turkish saber, that I use of a brisk morning when I charge off to work for the good of my neighbor; the street, shallow as a gutter, where I weave on Sunday walks with the family; the street, familiar as the way to school, where I sometimes tack my wobbly course, shameful to confess, in the small hours after partaking of alcohol.

Warsaw's New World Avenue is my universe, and also a small comet with a modest tail in that universe of mine.

Debacle

It happened right at the start. Not so long ago it used to come my way once a month or once in three weeks. Now every other day. The thirteenth Friday. Implosive slump.

Slump at the first pages of a book that was started without confidence or conviction. Perhaps one could work up some decent point, end the book right now, and then wait for death. But where do you go for a decent point? We are completely out of good points. The old ones are out of stock, and Providence is not producing new ones.

My life is made up of very short, low takeoffs and deep, long-lasting crawls. But who cares about that. Everyone is concerned with his own takeoff or painful slump.

Right now, a hundred thousand writers all over the world are pushing pen over paper in an effort to outdo Shakespeare and Dostoevsky.

Three million four hundred thousand quacks, health faddists, faith healers are straining every nerve in a mighty resolve to perform a miracle.

Four billion eight hundred million people are poring over horoscopes and waiting for happiness.

Debacle. Slavic, European, worldwide.

New World Avenue, Continued

The continuation of New World Avenue toward the Old Town is Krakowskie Przedmieście; in the direction of the royal palace of Wilanow, it is Aleje Ujazdowskie. This is where I have spent half my life. Circles, squares, churches, decaying shops, cafés and restaurants given to sudden death from consumption. A modest little quarter of a provincial town. The touching homestead of a provincial artist.

So I began my career on the stony cadaver of a murdered city. My new world—the great European world, to me, when I came here from my native Wilno country—consisted of a dozen or so bullet-riddled buildings and an enormous mass of basements, cellars, collapsing little storage sheds, caves black with soot, tunnels stinking of moldering corpses. This new world did not overwhelm me by its great scale, cultural splendor, or outlandish vitality. This new world, haunted by poverty like the villages of Belorussia, exalting in its proud emptiness like the virgin forest north of the Niemen, now had about it the stench of cinders like the little towns around Wilno.

It is only now, when I keep looking back, when I cast my eye more and more often beyond myself, that I begin to think of my literary contemporaries who at that time, somewhere in the world, tried to arrange words into sentences, and sentences into whole books. The world seemed enormous then and infinite, as it were, but today I know, and have had occasion to verify, too, that it is terribly small, so that it is a wonder that so many people find room in it and nobody falls off into the dread chill darkness of the sky—for the sky, to our universal consternation, has proved to be a frigid emptiness. Thus simply recalling those years, when we started living again and in a new way, makes me think more and more, as though about natural-born brothers, of those writers who are a little older or younger than I or actual contemporaries, of Joseph Heller or Philip Roth, of Kundera or Hrabal, of Stoppard or Pinter, of Aksyonov or Viktor Nekrasov. I don't know why, but I suddenly have the feeling that they are my kin: that I have been seeing sexologists with Roth, shivered in the trenches of Stalingrad with Nekrasov, traveled to India with Stoppard, waited with Vasya Aksyonov in Magadan for his mama, Eugenia Ginzburg, to get out of camp.

Something of the sort came over me abruptly and made me feel a sudden fellowship with the people who like myself, God knows why, arrange words into endless strings, and I came to feel a closeness to them, an affectionate solidarity, a sense of shared fate—though I don't know if that familiarity and brotherliness of mine will be at all welcome.

But when I return to that new world of Warsaw, meaning when I scramble in my memory over long barrows of hot plaster and glowing fragments of brick, when I halt among vast shrubberies of notchweed, thistle, and wormwood, and when I think of my unknown, as yet unlived destiny, then I call these young people from the distant future as witnesses. To witness what? Our shared defeats or individual victories? To witness what?

Slave of Empire, Head of Empire

New World Avenue, Warsaw, all Poland was then ruled by Czytelnik, the publishing cooperative founded by Borejsza. I don't know who Borejsza was, I don't know what he had done during the war. I got acquainted with him only in '47, when he moved *Rebirth* from Cracow to Warsaw. Why did this massive, chunky man with dry foam in the corners of his mouth, giving himself such characteristic airs, with the manners of a backwoods squire and the attitude of the all-powerful company boss of the early century; why did this man cast his sights on a modest literary weekly; why did he invest all his ambition in taking this plaything from Karol Kuryluk, the founder and creator of *Rebirth*; why, having several dozen dailies, weeklies, and monthlies, did he absolutely insist on running this smallish periodical?

Borejsza's empire held the whole country firmly in its paws: print shops, publishing houses, newspapers, mobile lending li-

braries, lecture societies, paper mills, too, I shouldn't wonder. I remember that in '48 Czytelnik even revived the "Tour of Poland" bicycle race. From the fourth-floor window on Wiejska, the street where the editorial office of *Rebirth* was located and which also belonged to the concern, I watched a cavalcade of contestants in colorful jerseys sway on their bikes down below, while Director Kobus, wearing the little white cap of the Bicyclists' Association, gave the starting signal with a large flag. But perhaps Director Kobus, head of transportation at Czytelnik, was merely in charge of organizing the race, while the signal for a fair start came from the president? I don't know, I don't remember; I remember only the sideways teetering of the racers, who braced themselves on one leg waiting for the start, and myself leaning out the office window into the sunny, or perhaps overcast, August day.

It was Borejsza's sole desire, his veritable craving, to be editor of *Rebirth*. Eventually, after some time, he satisfied it. Among a great many truly important functions he began to manage the affairs of a literary magazine. This was when I became his amanuensis, his factotum, his right hand—an invisible right hand. Barely of age, ill acquainted with literary matters, I edited *Re-*

birth with Borejsza's help. For I did in fact gradually become the all-powerful figure in this enterprise. When I used to walk into Borejsza's front office with ink-damp proof sheets, the platoons of secretaries male and female, department heads, directors would divide before me. Coolly, loftily, I would enter the office of the imperial Chief of Staff, where cabinet ministers awaiting an audience were meekly sitting on little chairs; I would go into that hushed room and, without a word, not wasting a glance on the jealous ministers, make for the door of the imperial inner sanctum with an authoritative stride, open it casually, and plunge into the off-limits interior.

As often as not, Borejsza would be behind a screen, receiving injections in his leg and mighty buttock.

"What's the hassle this time, Tadek?" he scolded between groans, tormented by the nurses.

"The columns are made up," I would say nonchalantly.

He would pull up his trousers, hurry to his desk, and begin to savor the menu of his beloved weekly. Sometimes he would dial a number and give voice in a negligent grunt: "Listen, Józek, what do you think of this . . ."

We, his assistants, knew he was calling the Prime Minister, Józef Cyrankiewicz. For our Caesar was a snob. He liked to be a ruler himself and to enter into alliances with rulers.

Come to think of it, though, I had got to know Borejsza much earlier; not so much to know, actually, as to see. It was in a dramatic and threatening situation in Cracow in '46, a very stormy year for that city, which distinguished itself by patriotic demonstrations on Constitution Day, the third of May. Well then, that summer or early autumn, I don't remember the exact time, a strike broke out at the national printing plant, where *Rebirth* was typeset and made up. I remember the moment when Borejsza, who had flown down by military plane from Warsaw, came into the page-making shop. He entered alone, without bodyguard, with a look of anger on his face, went in with the heavy step of a bulky man, and climbed up on a rickety, ink-stained stool of sorts. I watched him without sympathy, I didn't know anything about him as yet; to me he was a representative of the regime, come to suppress a workers' strike.

He did not speak more than twenty minutes; and it wasn't a

speech by a Party functionary. The typesetters and page-makers were addressed by the head of a big company, a man who had the good of the firm and its workers at heart. I don't remember his words or arguments, but I do remember that the strike at this print shop ended at once, and boss and workmen went off to their respective callings in amity. And it should be noted that those times did not favor easy accords.

Yes—Borejsza was a phenomenon which that era had no need of. Yes—Borejsza was a genius of a sort, whom his own system rejected. Yes—Borejsza was already doomed to fall that first moment when he ascended the stairs of the empire founded by him.

But he wasn't aware of this. He imagined (saving your presence, Mr. Censor) that socialism, which was taking on substance before our eyes, needed human intelligence, dash, judicious initiative, and a tolerant understanding for the human failings, past and present, which action constantly breeds.

I, now, was a freedman, an escapee at his court in those days. That was a pretty apt description for one who, like me, had left the woods of Wilno behind two or three years before and taken a nosedive into the depths of Europe—already Eastern, to be sure, already peoplesrepublicated. Hence I was an escapee from political rights, or better, from the political oppression that was my due for the recent past, and I was a social, perhaps even class escapee, who had leapt from a kolkhoz near Wilno straight into international reception rooms, where one rubbed sleeves with Picasso, Eluard, Aldous Huxley, and Pablo Neruda.

Then, an escapee, I cruised with impunity and universal toleration all over the palaces of the Czytelnik organization. I rode in the president's Horch, an enormous limousine which had belonged to Göring or Himmler. That monster had an infinite number of cylinders, and its engine looked like the power plant of a bomber. In that machine I swished about the streets of Warsaw; for longer distances there was a dark-green, lurid-looking Dakota.

I was *Rebirth*'s editorial secretary. Educated and trained by Kuryluk, I was eminently well versed in the technology of periodical production, I knew in my sleep all the intricacies of orthography and grammar; awakened at midnight, I could locate in minutes, in old prewar bound volumes of *Literary News*, a line drawing of Paul Valéry or a halftone picture of Bernard Shaw. The enterprise called *Rebirth* could not function without me. I knew all its secrets, all its frailties and neuralgic points.

I am not being boastful when I say that some of my colleagues obtained lucrative positions from my hands, others received help through my editing a miserable novel or a volume of less than profound verse. I was somebody in those days, although I didn't know that the vessel on which I rummaged about so lightheartedly was already leaky and slowly going to the bottom.

It is not true that Borejsza began to sicken, that he fell into a fatal decline after a car accident. He was doomed from the very start by the laws of the system whose idol is—my humble apologies, Mr. Censor—the anonymous apparatchik, the gray mouse lording it in the darkness backstage. The impenetrable structure of interdependencies.

Hapless *Rebirth* was the opium allaying the suffering of a dying cultural dictator, who in the wrong era and with the wrong timing found himself in a country which was rising from lethargy to a tragic life.

Pronouns

When I found myself in a new world—or, shall I say, when I landed on New World Avenue—a strong, prewar sun still shone, which acted like a furnace on the cracked brickwork, the rusty overhead girders, and the thick dust that rose and settled over this vast torrid cemetery. I said the sun was still prewar, for that's what it really was. The woods were prewar, the clouds were, and so were the rivers. That is to say, they were still themselves, unspoiled by man. The world was different by then, changed, or even new, but nature carried over into these approaching times, this new dimension of reality, in its primeval shape.

I have trouble recalling those late forties; it seems to me that a bright, kindly sun always shone from a clear sky at that time. And I see myself lying on the couch in my smallish room on Frascati Street, staring at the ceiling, horribly bored in my solitude, bored throughout my spare time, sometimes from dawn to nightfall. These were times marked by extraordinary tedium, like being isolated in a decompression chamber before a new life stage. Boredom, for that matter, is the bane of my life in any case. All of me is one big boredom gland. Boredom has formed my character, my habits, and doubtless my intellectual makeup. I am a vast wound of boredom. I am an epileptic wave of boredom, bound for who knows where.

I have such a difficult time recalling those years. They are lodged in my memory as a sudden whiff of fragrance, a flash of light, or a fragment of a tune. Stirred by these, they abruptly rise from oblivion, and I feel a sort of delicious ache or, better, a blithe distress. I am astonished by the terrible distance between myself of that time and myself today. It makes for a sort of superstitious terror in me, although I know that it is merely an alteration of the chemistry of my organism, the proportions of chemical elements changing; yet perhaps not only that: perhaps I am drawing near to that wailing wall beyond which lies the unknown. So I thought back ruefully on that trek through time or through the dimension allotted us, I brought it up in my *Moonrise, Moonset*, and promptly the snoopers fired off reports to the effect that I was using my youth for an excuse, trying to lie my way out of sinful years past and to pacify them, those moral gumshoes of mine, and smooth their feathers. The hell with them! As if I didn't have better things to do than to bend an ear to their wretched pantings behind my back!

It is a failure, though. I have fallen down and will never rise again. I know about it, I remember it even in my sleep. I wake up before dawn with my pulse racing and think of this cellar, whose black walls I see about me all the time. This last affliction is the turn of pronouns. I have been through afflictions adjectival and adverbial, and now the pronominal is upon me. Out of the quagmires, the marshes of pronouns, there is no escape. Pronouns will sift all over me and bury me forever.

The Mystery Reader

One day there came to the editorial offices a smartly dressed gentleman, whom Kuryluk ushered into his study with considerable ceremony. They conversed behind closed doors for some time; at last Kuryluk appeared and with that always meaning smile of his asked me: "Would you mind joining us?"

I stepped into the editor's study; the elegant gentleman rose from the armchair.

"Here is Tadzio Konwicki in the flesh," said the editor.

It turned out that I had been introduced to Leon Kruczkowski, who had just resigned the office of vice-minister of culture but still flaunted the ministerial aura. Kruczkowski invited me to his apartment for a chat.

I learned that he had read my *Marshes* for the publishing house and decided to have a look at the young author. Kuryluk whispered to me that the reader was inclined in my favor, but the publishers had serious reservations.

On the appointed day I hurried to pay my visit to the cabinet member-cum-literatus. The place probably was in Aleja Róż, Rose Lane, for I remember a shaded study with rare dapples of sun on the floor and the walls, I remember the impressive affluence of the apartment, and a bottle of sorts. I spent several hours in that study, but am able to recall very little of it. Kruczkowski must have sat in the easy chair and looked at me, and I at him. We did not talk a great deal. His somewhat waxen face with heavy bags under the eyes struck me as a genuinely literary countenance and intimidated me greatly. I believe he paid me a few compliments at the beginning; frugally, though, and without commitment. We may have had something to drink, too, but not a lot. After that, Kruczkowski unleashed his tongue; only in his own terms, of course. He unloaded slow, rare sentences, while I listened politely.

What he seemed to be telling me was the contents of a novel he was planning or working on. He reported the plot to me in some detail and was quite meticulous about its climax. The narrative gave me pause, it seemed so melodramatic and sentimental. Politics was tightly interlaced with amorous or, rather, conjugal vicissitudes. Possibly the author inscribed triangles or squares into the geometry of the Party, I can't quite recall now, at the bottom of my memory there winks only a scene featuring the hero of the book or drama making a very important speech from the rostrum of a hall, while somewhere behind the scenes palpitates his personal tragedy.

At that time I was still fairly distant from political affairs and the Party. I listened to this confession from a remove, mildly gripped in my mind by the circumstances, a bit staggered by those compliments, the liquid refreshment, and the lack of prospects for my maiden book. I did leave that study in a state of some consternation, though, over the confessions of a living classic, confessions which made me, as it were, the confidant and intimate colleague of a writer who was my senior by at least a generation.

In later times I have been unable to find in his writings any trace of this literary nugget as described to me by Kruczkowski. Perhaps I did not search or read with sufficient zeal. What always strikes me about the whole episode, though, is that Kruczkowski never spoke a word to me in the subsequent twenty years until his death, never gave me a hint that he remembered that rather intimate encounter years earlier, or ever acknowledged in so many words my presence in literature.

The Curse of Resemblances

In my time there was a surfeit of philosophers. When I say "in my time" I mean the period before that vast moral catastrophe incident upon World War II. But that catastrophe, that great earthquake, that global cataclysm, that event unheard of in human history occurred not during the war, not in the aftermath of the war, but only in the late fifties and early sixties. This outburst was a case of delayed ignition, occurring after a certain

time, upon reflection, or simply in the course of collecting one's thoughts. As late as fifteen years after the last murder of a man by another, after the last incineration of a man by another, only then did everything come crashing down. Not all at once, of course, at one moment, in the winking of an eye. It began to break down imperceptibly, but in the fifteen years that followed, it collapsed totally. All kinds of discipline, all hierarchies, taboos, sanctities were ground to dust and trodden into the patient soil. By way of punishment. Punishment for the crime of genocide.

Before this came about, though, our world, our peaceable God's world was swarming with philosophers. Every other doctor was a Ph.D. But now, if you ran into one it would only be in Germany; the Germans have always been a bit shameless.

These days the philosophers, who used to be so impudent and arrogant, hide behind innocent designations like sociologist, psychologist, medievalist, sexologist, even parapsychologist or radio-esthetist. The philosophers feel guilty, suffer a sense of responsibility for that chain of years between 1939 and 1945, for those two thousand days which the world, humanity, perhaps even the Lord God will never forget. It takes a lot of courage to pronounce oneself a philosopher today.

The ones who stole the philosophers' daily bread are the minstrels. More precisely, the lyricists, shifty old foxes who supply the youth groups with songs. What is done in these songs is totally to leach out, thoroughly drag through the mud, dishonor beyond return all possible aspects of philosophy, ontology, eschatology, cosmogony. For cash, for a sip of fame, for the momentary intoxication of a feral divinity, teenage guitarists and aging graphomaniacs have peed on everything that is contained between nativity and mortal agony, between life and death. Daily, hundreds of thousands of dung beetles, earthworms, and ants root in the wretched tumulus of existence allotted us who knows by whom for who knows how long.

However, I am not a philosopher, I have no philosophers in the family and suffer no pain from this calamity. I have a different affliction. What riles me is another misfortune, which was brought forth by that same earthquake, or perhaps by the setup of the solar system as such. I smart, writhe, and agonize under the curse of resemblances. I resemble all of you, bright and dumb, great and small, saints and sinners. I resemble you to the point that I have hardly formed a thought when I already find it in you. I can hardly write a word before seeing it written by someone else. Barely do I start my death agony when I see one just like it next to me.

We resemble each other like cats or sparrows. We react in the same way to a morsel of food, the attack of a rival, the sexual signals of a female. All our art is one great cyclical threshing over of one and the same material, which is contained between the electric excitation of lifeless matter and its return to extinction. Which finds room in the poor, unresourceful, uninteresting, perhaps even faultily designed existence of two-legged mammals.

For so many ages we played with that naïve solace, personality. For so many eras docile philosophers instilled in us a belief in our godlike qualities, lured us with the magic of genius, held out the omnipotence of the demiurges.

Whereas we barely made it as far as concrete caves, a capacity for flawed long-distance communication, and somewhat faster locomotion than that afforded by our feet. And the only divine gift that we possessed ourselves of is the gift of killing. The curse of resemblances. The resemblance of curses. At this instant, several thousand pen gnawers in varied recesses of this minute planet are threatening and scolding philosophers, and in this same moment, thousands of basically identical bipedal mammals suffer tortures over the humiliating, hopeless, appalling curse of resemblances.

The Blinstrubs

When I settled on New World Avenue, the Blinstrubs took turns dying in the Wilno Colony. First Uncle Blinstrub, then Aunt Blinstrub. Actually, they weren't my uncle and aunt. They were my great-uncle and great-aunt. By our usage it wouldn't do, though, to antiquate one's more distant relations, hence for this degree of kinship the proper address was "aunt" and "uncle." Aunt Blinstrub my grandmother's sister, who, along with her five sisters, was descended from the Pieślaks, who were settled at Krzyżówka, a manorial grange somewhere Niemen way. Now, I understand, the road through the center of Krzyżówka has become the frontier between the republics of Lithuania and Belorussia. The aunts who have traveled there report that the inhabitants on the Lithuanian side have remained Poles, while those on the Belorussian side have been registered as Belorussians. It's not important, anyway. There are few of those Pieślaks left by now.

After the confiscations following the Uprising of 1863, the Blinstrubs, robbed of their patrimony, went into tenant farming. Their last holding was the manorial grange of Tupaciszki. After World War I, when independence was restored to the country,

the owner subdivided the land into small parcels. Those pic-
turesquely situated overlooking the valley of the Wilenka were
bought up chiefly by the railroad men, but a good many went
to the more well-to-do among the Wilno civil servants, local
notables, as well as people of prominence in government who
were originally from the Wilno area but had lost their native
haunts there.

My uncle—Great-uncle Blinstrub, Przemysław by name, was
left with a few parcels of land scattered along the lower Wilno
Colony. For there were two Wilno Colonys, a lower one along
the railroad over the riverside leas and an upper one on the
wooded plateau which overhangs the valley.

The reason I wanted so badly to think back to the Blinstrubs
was that whenever I reach for a book of reminiscences of Lithuania, of the lands of the old historic Lithuania, I immediately
come upon the name of Blinstrub. Be they the memoirs of the
famous Father Meysztowicz or the tales of Wańkowicz, or simply some collections of documents—everywhere I find refer-
ences to this old Lithuanian? Belorussian? Swedish? family. I
myself don't know which, and never had an opportunity to
search for the roots of this clan. As a boy I rummaged a little
in the old papers of the Pieślaks, and also of the Blinstrubs. I

was already aware that both belonged to the nobility, and the papers testifying to this had been well preserved. In the old days, if you weren't a nobleman—what the Russians called a *dvoryanin*, you went into the Tsar's army for a twenty-five-year term. In many civilized countries this is now the highest criminal punishment.

There is a curious and noteworthy circumstance about the Wilno country: to the very end, that is, to our end in 1945, topographical names were not normalized. Differences also showed up in surnames: Blinstrub was often spelled Blinstrup. This was due to the fact that, through endless decades, this neck of the woods floundered in the darkness spread by the tsarist government, in backwardness and outright illiteracy. This *severozapadny kray*—or Russian "northwestern border"—was Russified and Ruthenianized by the Russian rulers and flooded with the Orthodox religion, while it continually rebelled and stubbornly gnawed the bit. But as a result of fairly general illiteracy, owing to the absence of the written word, all names, appellations, and clannish labels spread and passed down the generations "by ear," that is, in a deceptive and transient oral shape.

Our little river Wilenka was called "Wilejka" to the end of the interwar Republic, and actually almost everyone calls it Wilejka to this day; while I, who was born on its banks, know that "Wilenka" is the proper form.

But now that it is springtime, I want to recall my grandparents Blinstrub, for April 13 is Great-uncle Przemysław's name day; and I want to commemorate them, seeing that I was their prodigal son, almost prodigal grandson, collateral scion, fosterling. In May 1945, I left for "Poland" and was never heard from again. I did actually give a timid sign of life or two in the Stalin era, when communication between Wilno and the mother country practically died down completely. I must have sent some sort of a letter now and then, but they died without having much of an idea what happened to Tadźka. There was nobody to tell them in time where their foster son had landed and what he was doing, and if it had been worth it to make sacrifices for him so many years, to take food from their own mouths, to push him through school, through unsuitable habits, sudden fits

Aunt Blinstrub against the churches of St. Ann,
the Bernardines, and St. Michael's

of dandyism; to force him among people and toward a clouded, strange, ill-omened future.

My grandmother was a Pieślak by birth. Those Pieślaks, it seems, nourished ambitions and probably did not make poor marriages. My Great-aunt Malwina always comes across in my memory as dark-haired with a first touch of silver, not exactly good-looking, but with a lively, intelligent face, a certain charm, a certain talent for communicating and dealing with people, an aristocratic sense of honor, and a noblewoman's ambition. It is to her I owe the most, if I have anything to owe in my shoddy life. It was she who invested all her unfulfilled expectations, hopes, and ambitions in me, the so-called orphan child turned over to the family to be raised after his father's death; in a six-year-old boy who—embarrassing to admit—was something of a crybaby; and who found himself one day in the Wilno Colony, in its phase of most explosive growth in the early thirties, in the care of people not far from old age, the childless Blinstrub couple, his great-uncle and great-aunt.

Uncle Przemysław was of medium stature, slender, not to say

thin as a rail from work. He had a very handsome face distinguished by a hawk nose and adorned by a Polish mustache, a face worthy of a senator of the ancient Polish-Lithuanian Commonwealth. A dimwitted and rather scatterbrained boy though I was, I still came to think early on that Uncle Przemysław was a handsome man and could be President, or at least Marshal.

The branch of the Blinstrubs Uncle Przemysław was descended from was already greatly impoverished; we might even simply say, sunk into the peasant class. Scraps of aristocratic pretensions yet remained, there still lay in old wardrobes baronial instruments of conferment, still, from somewhere, contempt for boorishness would emerge all of a sudden; but after all, here was a baron who himself plowed the soil, sowed his bit of rye, and in the wintertime threshed from three or four in the morning.

Uncle Blinstrub almost never spoke. Talk, according to his firm conviction, was vacuity, time-wasting blather unworthy of a man. He had a certain store of proverbs, Russian ones for some reason, or perhaps Belorussian, which served him to meet all life's demands. "Afraid of the wolf—don't enter the forest." "It's not our business to bargain for butter, that's what we have clerks for." "Not a priest—don't wear the cloth." "Gentler you drive, farther you get." "When a dog has nothing to do, he licks his balls."

The interesting thing is that all the proverbs seem to flow from a somewhat defensive attitude toward life. They make a shibboleth of passivity, or perhaps merely sing the praises of moderation and restraint. Those golden (or silver-gilt) thoughts contained a certain fraction of Grandfather Blinstrub's philosophy of life. Not only of his philosophy, though, come to think of it: that limitation of scope, after all, and modest appetite for life were peculiar to all the strange people among whom, taking my time, I grew up over eighteen years. On the other hand, all these people, though not particularly well educated, differed enormously from each other. When I now fulminate against the curse of resemblances, I overlook the awful plague I left behind, among the people who stayed on the sunny opposite bank, where everyone was an original, an eccentric, a unique handiwork of the Lord.

Grandmother Malwina and Grandfather Przemysław met and

married very late. She was already going on fifty, and he must have been well past sixty. Here I am suddenly reminded that, rummaging in yellowed birth certificates, I once came across Grandfather Przemysław's birth date, a date I have never forgotten since. He was born in 1865, two years after the Uprising, and evidently grew up under the auspices of that unhappy rift. The Uprising was evidently stamped into his consciousness, his character, and his views; and this same event, still fresh, as it were, unfaded, full of tumult, weeping, and carbine salvos, I took over from him and carried within me, as he did, bore it through the partisan struggle, the war, and all the upheavals right up to this day; and every night I hear the knock at the window, which is the agreed sign, and start up with my heart pounding, start up to nothing, just the dejection of the small hours, the heartache of approaching age.

That is probably why they didn't have children—they got married late in life. However, there must have been such a fashion at the time, for my father, too, got married just a few years before his death. I mentioned something about Grandfather Przemysław's taciturnity awhile ago. The fact is that I don't remember his ever addressing me. I don't mean that he didn't sometimes mutter a monosyllable, even a particular word; but I definitely never heard from his lips a whole sentence addressed to me, with subject and predicate. As a rule he communicated with me like a deaf-and-dumb person. He showed me by a gesture what I was to do. Sometimes, when he was dissatisfied with me, he gave a low grunt. When it was time for a hiding, I knew myself that one had to go to that certain place by the wall where the whip hung and await the merited punishment.

Grandmother Malwina, by the way, was a good interpreter and would often give expression to her husband's thoughts and decisions regarding myself. In those years I was a bit of a rascal, not in the least resembling a homeless orphan. Aware of Grandmother's indulgence, her warm heart and fervent affection for her fosterling, I allowed myself some escapades which even now, after so many years, I am reluctant to bring up. Grandmother, enjoying her well-earned rest in heaven, has forgotten them, I am sure, and I don't see any reason to return to those matters.

I write about grandparents who weren't my grandparents, after all; I write about them and cannot part from them, because for years, for decades by now, my conscience has been gnawing at me. I left them behind there, alone, old, isolated, perhaps embittered by my ingratitude; and at a certain time I began recalling them on every occasion, figuring that my belated regret might redeem my guilt.

And so at the present moment, as I am returning to New World Avenue, I am not taking leave from them yet, for I haven't said everything I meant to say. I am going to visit them again as they lie there in their graves on a wooded slope, from which one can see the whole great vale of the Wilenka, the city of Wilno, where the little river debouches, and the distant vapors behind which the world lies in wait, this world in its wretchedness; and I, middle-aged, melancholy, disenchanted, am in this world for no purpose I can see.

And right at this moment I thought with envy of my avuncular grandparents, the Blinstrubs. I had always thought of them with a kind of shamefaced compassion. I pitied them for having worked so hard all their lives, and for their lives having been gray, drab, very frugal, lacking amusements, comforts, sudden turns of fortune, colorful adventures, great achievements in the social or intellectual sphere. On my high perch I had even felt to blame in a way for their hopeless life. Then one day all of a sudden the idea entered my head that they had perhaps been happier than I, who had traveled half the world by air, experienced one thing and another, got skin-tight with all the things I had read about, with my heart in my throat, in the Wilno Colony. And suddenly I envied them their hard life of toil, marked by duties, discipline, stern customs, and their sole recreation, which was the daily prayer.

My Threats

I don't write the truth. I write half-truths of a sort, curlicues, periphrases, concealments by silence, utterances of spurious candor, pretended openness. I produce all this fearful literary noise, foam whipped up on the river of facts, a vast fog in which we blunder with outstretched hands.

Yet I am tortured by a need for truth, an overpowering hunger for it. All the time, morning and evening, I think of how I might go about expressing my truth, that is, what I really think of you people, how I view my colleagues, how I look upon our common destiny. And I am telling you, one day, at a suitable moment, I am going to unload all this and let it stand as testimony, when the future comes, to myself, to us, to our time.

Note that for the last two centuries all the better and more genuine Polish literature was created far from Poland. From Mickiewicz to Gombrowicz. It was born where there was no Polish hayseed and obscurant, no congenital idiot, no pestering chauvinist. Note that only abroad could a Polish writer wield the pen in freedom, speak his mind boldly and bluntly about his own society and himself, immerse himself without complexes in the tide of common global thought—where he is not at the mercy of the collective blackmail of an exasperated but obtuse, tragic but untutored, pitiful but arrogant native society.

At this point my caveman compatriot will raise a howl and run off to write an abusive anonymous letter. But I can't help things being as they are. Such is the state of affairs, and many facts document it. Isn't it true that in an uncouth and indolent society like ours readers have beaten up literary men? Not a despot, not a censor, not a policeman, but student romantics beat up Bolesław Prus, crippling him for life. And Nowaczyński with his eye knocked out? And the massacred Wilno publicist Cywiński? And Słonimski, whom they slapped?

Our poor, anemic, barely breathing literature, badgered from all sides—how timid, polite, and ingratiating it was; yet it stung numskulls not only from government circles but also from that sacred and fervid brotherhood, the patriotic rabble.

There is no literature without reader. Like reader, like literature. The reader is accountable for the level of our verse and narrative. It is not true that *spiritus flat ubi vult*, the spirit bloweth whither it listeth. The flame of genuine literature is kindled only where the philistine and the yahoo don't extinguish the first feeble sparklet.

However—I am not going to make a mistake this time. In this book I am not going to draw flattering portraits of living artists or tell heartwarming anecdotes about colleagues I like. All my panegyrics so far have been met by roars of rage from those portrayed. My hair stood on end—what was left of it— at this brutal demonstration of hypersensitive vanity, towering presumption, and unbridled conceit. Only those I cuffed or pinched reacted with truly benevolent moderation. Only they passed over my growls and barks and returned to the order of business.

This is why at this point I bend my knees in deep contrition and cast my tearful gaze at two wonderful Stefans who reign over today's Poland: Kisielewski, ruler of the simple tribe of columnists, and Bratkowski, dictator of Polish journalism. I gaze at them with affection and groan with inward pangs for having dared to poke their respectable plumpitudes in one of my pamphlets. Woe is me, woe . . .

The Cat Ivan

At times someone will inquire of me about the cat Ivan's health, or ask quite directly whether the cat Ivan is still living. The animal has a number of devoted friends, and also a handful of worshippers. Not wishing to boast, I may let out in an undertone that in times of crisis there used to arrive for the cat Ivan from various parts of the world appetizing little packages with exquisite feline tidbits. It must be admitted that these gifts aroused fierce jealousy in the breasts of the remaining members of the household. Even I was none too well pleased when I had lugged a heavy parcel from the post office and on unpacking it found that it was full of cans of cat food.

The cat Ivan is already a distinctly elderly gentleman. Early in July of this year he will observe his birthday, two weeks after mine. We were both born under the sign of Cancer, you see.

The cat Ivan will complete fifteen years, which on the feline scale of life expectancy is an extremely mature age indeed.

What about my aged friend's looks? Without bias, one must concede that he keeps in fine shape and truly doesn't look more than ten years old. His coat is still thick and furry, with a strong tinge of cinnamon along his belly. His eye is lively, beautiful, variegated with subtle hues. His whiskers are still full and beetling, Marshal Piłsudski caliber. His posture is imposing, his movements energetic, even if he no longer jumps lightly from the table but trickles cautiously down a leg.

Yes, it is true, Ivan is no youngster anymore. Above all, hunting is over with. No longer does he triumphantly bring in a sparrow in his teeth from the balcony. Far from it—he is even afraid now to go out on the balcony by himself. When he forgets and glides out, blinking into the sun and probing the spring air with the tips of his whiskers, instantly a fierce squeal of bird calls rises up on every hand, from every tree, pillar, and pole. Presently squadrons of sparrows come whirring up and dive-bomb the innocent creature with a horrid rattle, hem him in, call him names like murderer and war criminal as likely as not; and poor Ivan moans quietly to himself and, humiliated, annihilated, streaks back into the room. He complains, whimpers, skulks in corners, cursing his fall, while on the balcony the sparrows celebrate a triumph. They settle on the railing and tell each other in shrieks how they routed the Cat.

The cat Ivan does not go out on the balcony except with us. I have to shield him from the ruthless aggression of the little birds, those poor runts which ten years ago the cat Ivan used to chivy and swat like flies, to the point that, but for my intervention, he would have extirpated the bird population of the entire street, perhaps even of the whole of Warsaw.

The above, unfortunately, does not mean in the least that the cat Ivan makes allowances for us. Quite the contrary: he seems to use us to work off his frustration in the matter of birds. I myself, to be sure, answer every brutal act with equal brutality and therefore suffer less from the old predator. But my ladies are in a bad way. My wife, as in years past, gets assaulted in dark passages for the smallest misstep. Now it is that the milk is not up to par, because the farmers add laundry powder; another time it is that the fish is not first-rate, or that it's high time there was roast beef again. Oh, yes—you can read to the cat Ivan from *Trybuna Ludu*, the organ of the Party, for hours at a time, but he won't be convinced by the most brilliant publicist. He has his requirements, and *basta*.

Right now night is closing in. I am lying on the couch, as is my custom, a writing pad propped against the knees of my drawn-up legs, and guide my old fountain pen over the paper, describing my friend, who is lost somewhere and hasn't shown up for some time. I know, though, that he is snoozing in an easy chair, not by any chance the one made up for him, but a totally different one, which tomorrow will look like the den of a balding fox. That is where he snoozes persistently, but when he senses that I am sleepy, he emerges from the gloom by my couch, stretches first his front paws, then his hind ones, yawns once more with that crafty expression of his old muzzle, and, insensitive to my protests, leaps treacherously onto my blanket-covered stomach, quickly settles down, and begins to purr, so as to say that things are exactly right, that we should lie like this for a few hours until he gets tired of it, that he enjoys listening to my pulse, and that we are real friends after all. And I tolerate this, I have to stand it. I turn on the radio, think of various unpleasant matters, chiefly about the fact that this year was to be the year of the Cancer sign, when nothing but extraordinary things were to come my way from everywhere, all sorts of lucky strokes and unlooked-for successes . . . which were indeed coming my way, but all of a sudden skipped aside somewhere, jumping to the Rams, Lions, Scorpios, or Capricorns, leaving us, the cat Ivan and myself, in a jam, an anathema or pickle, in something like a glob of aspic without taste or smell.

The cat lies sprawled on my remains. At times a shudder or something like a spasm runs over him; suddenly he will give a tiny moan, then shake a paw as if to flick off something that had stubbornly stuck to his warm, soft, black little pads. The cat Ivan is dreaming. But what he dreams, where he directs his rays, and what reply he receives from that dimension or reality

the cat Ivan on my belly

where the cats hold sway, I don't know. But I do know that, in spite of everything, regardless of tensions, of rows over the rolled-up newspaper I sometimes use, that for all that the cat Ivan is well-disposed toward us, and that this goodwill of his will prove our salvation when at a certain hour we cross the boundary of our reality and find ourselves beyond, in a different universe unknown to us, where, who knows, cats may wield great influence and hold a tremendous position.

Holy Saturday

I was ten, perhaps eleven years old at the time. I was hanging around the sideboard in the sacristy where the priest was donning the vestments for Holy Mass. There were a lot of altar boys in that narrow and gloomy place that day. Once a year you get so many boys in surplices assembled in one place, and that time is Holy Saturday, yes, definitely Holy Saturday; although my memory for detail is erratic and sometimes I think it was Good Friday. No, it couldn't have been Good Friday, for I was in charge of the Paschal, after all, the thick Easter candle with pinecones worked into it in memory of the wounds of Christ. I am not going to check this, it isn't even proper for me to check it, so I am deciding that the action took place on Holy Saturday of a cloudy Easter before the war. Holy Saturday is practically the holidays, so we were pleasurably excited, fidgeting and buzzing about and elbowing each other in that sacristy, acolytes and celebrants as we all were, and I with that Paschal. At this point, though, I am assailed by doubts as to whether this could have been on Saturday; perhaps it was on Friday after all, when there is the greatest crowd in the church and the most elaborate liturgy.

However! It doesn't matter in the end which day it was. What matters is that I was prancing alongside the sideboard with that thick candle near the door which led to the presbytery, and at a certain moment, so as not to be put to shame by my fellows, who were making faces behind the priest's back and blowing smoke signals with incense, I raised that Paschal like a rifle and "presented arms" with it.

At that moment the priest stopped his robing, strode up to me, took the candle away, and put it down on the top of the sideboard; then he seized me by the neck, dragged me to the door which led to the courtyard, opened it, and flung me down the stairs. It was just as you have read it many times in novels and heard tell in anecdotes: "He was cast down the stairs."

The door slammed, separating me forever from the sacristy,

the censer, the missal, the giggles in the corners, the pride of crimson capes, that initiation at an altar divided from the faithful, that is, friends, schoolfellows, relations, by a balustrade covered with a white cloth. The door slammed with a crash, as if the sky had collapsed on me. For quite a while I waited—on the ground? kneeling? squatting?—for all this to unhappen. But it didn't.

So I got up, took off the surplice, which I would never again have use for now, and made for home by way of a wooded slope. To this day, after almost fifty years, I see myself pick my way, stooped and with the folded surplice under my arm, along that track among the trees, the steep little path propelling me irresistibly down, while I dig my heels in, trying to slow down and delay my return home.

Many are the times I have reflected on that rather insignificant episode so many years in the past. Everyone has in his life's history stacks of similar misadventures, peccadillos, transgressions. I was guilty, I had played the fool with the candle, had failed to maintain the gravity due the feast day, which demanded from a person nothing but sorrow, regret, and contrition. I have taken the authorship of that escapade upon myself, and have many times thereafter described that priest in my books, paying him honor, reverent esteem, and admiration for his martyrdom after the war. Sometimes, though, like the serpents of Satan, pernicious zigzags of doubt have slithered into my mind, making me wonder why this holy man, later a true martyr of the faith, happened to pick on me out of the whole bunch of boys from the best families in the parish who were cutting up at the time; me, known as an orphan—and orphanhood in those days was the depth of misery.

Magnanimously I passed over this incident to the order of business, to an afterlife that made sense, or didn't, to acceptance of what Providence floated by and offered me. But there are moments when I wonder if that humiliation, the first downfall and loss in my life, if that far-off Easter Saturday left some trace in me, some blemish, something like a crack, which I was never able afterward to patch up or glue or paste over.

Resurrection

This was when I spent time in the rehabilitation ward of one of the Warsaw hospitals. It was autumn. A little sunlight filtered into our room, which contained four beds, of which one—the one next to mine, separated from it only by a cardiac resuscitation kit—was vacant. One bed was empty, and in the two beds opposite lay two elderly gentlemen; the older one had been wheeled in during my tenure here, and I had seen him being arranged in bed, taped up to monitors, connected to an IV line. I had seen him in pain at first, apparently unconscious, then slowly coming to—to an old man's precarious equilibrium, that is. On our right, like a hallway to our little ward, was a glass box with our monitor dials, in front of which, day and night, sat nurses, old ones and young ones, pretty and plain, lazy and busy. Sometimes doctors showed up; one particularly struck me because I seemed to sense something unmedical about him, something like an artistic intuition, a certain foreignness, or the mark of an arresting oddity. Moreover, he had a great bushy mattress of curly hair, which reminded me of something in my childhood or early adolescence, something far away, in the Wilno country, perhaps in Belorussia.

I, too, lay prostrate, immobile, taped all over with wires like a prewar radio. In the monitor over my head my personal zigzags leapt about, which I variegated by making more vehement movements or accelerating my breathing when no one was looking. I was content with myself and with the hospital routine. In fear, as I had been, of the various terrible and repulsive afflictions which lay in wait for me right and left now that old age was near, I now suddenly found myself in a convalescent ward with a heart condition—a handsome and romantic menace promising a swift, easy death.

So I lay there, satisfied with myself and merciful destiny, full of benevolence toward people, a pleasantly stimulated, cheerful, premature oldster. Then all of a sudden one morning, when our room was full of sun, they wheeled in on an oilcloth-covered gurney a rather carelessly shaven character, not young but not old, either, somewhere after the forty mark, I would say. They moved him over onto the bed, the sheet shifted, and I saw the powerful, still sunburned body and thought to myself, Man, there is a hunk for you, there's a fellow in pretty good health. The two other old men also inspected that mountain of muscle, sinews, and bones which, covered by a thin skin, lay on the white bedding.

The patient did not groan too much, just grumbled from time to time when they hooked monitors up to him; that curly-headed doctor of mine talked with him in an undertone, and I gathered that he had been brought in straight from some work-shop, that he was a mechanic or blacksmith. He seemed em-barrassed by his situation, complained of chest pains, but you could tell that he felt like flying the coop and would do it, too, the moment the pain subsided.

After a while the nurses left his side, and so did my doctor. Our room was still full of sunshine; quite as in summer, in July or August. I seemed to hear somewhere behind the wall water gurgling in a basin and children's cries. Both the old men started to nap, and the new patient also closed his lids. Only I was unable to sleep, because I was healthy and good health kept me from sleeping.

This being so, I watched that glass chamber containing the monitors. The nurses had sat down at the table again, the doctor had gone to his room. Presently he came back, shoved his hands into the deep pockets of his white gown in a movement char-acteristic of him, and exchanged some banter with the girls. They began to ask him for something, he nodded, and the dear girls, bustling like little white sparrows, went off for tea or a late breakfast. All was quiet. The new arrival was dozing, the old men were dozing, and I pretended I was, too. My doctor walked about the instrument chamber, glancing at the monitors, always with his hands in those pockets.

Suddenly he stopped, his eyes glued to the top left dial. In an almost imperceptible movement he had his hands out of the pockets and clapped them together. At this, the head of an R.N. showed in the door. He said something in a whisper which loosed a snowstorm. Five or six white girlish figures all of a sudden surrounded the new patient's bed.

The doctor said in a low tone: "We have twenty-four seconds."

I am not sure this was the number of seconds. But I seem to remember that he gave them a deadline of twenty-odd seconds. What happened then really defies description. In a single moment these girls shot an uncountable salvo of needles into the patient, and did other things to him, hustling and bustling around his inert body. This was really uncanny, and I shall never forget it, nor ever understand better the weight and onus of time. The doctor at this juncture pointed to that electric heart stimulator. A diminutive nurselet had it open in a flash, the doctor grabbed the electrodes and immediately said something in a choked voice. One of the girls repeated it more loudly: "The fuse is blown."

Now that little thing rushed into the corridor and practically in the same motion dragged into the space between our beds a portable machine which in normal conditions a weight lifter would have had trouble moving. The doctor seized these new electrodes, which looked like carbon-covered pipes ending in small plates, one blue, the other red, and applied these plates to the patient's chest. I heard a slight crack as the patient's heavy body leapt some two feet in the air with an inhuman sort of groan, a kind of yelp or hideous release of gas. But the outlandish, uncanny traffic continued, something was constantly being done; that body was gouged, pricked, tortured, outraged in order to return it to life.

"Once more," said the doctor quietly.

And again he applied those pipes to the mechanic's or smith's heart. And again that hundred eighty or two hundred pounds of dead meat leapt up with an appalling squeal. The bustle around him did not subside, grew more intense if anything; I have no way of telling how many injections were jabbed into muscles or veins, what was squeezed and what opened. For between those electric detonations my doctor exerted a rhythmic pressure against the patient's rib cage, as if it were the lid of some stubborn box that would not close for him.

"One more time," he whispered.

Once again that heavy body flew up with uncommon agility, and again it emitted that dreadful sound of death, torpor, dissolution, and shamelessness, a sound I shall never forget. The mechanic fell back onto the bedsheet, and suddenly everything slowed down. It was just like in a film when the pace returns to normal after a speed-up and becomes fluid, free, and natural. The nurses continued attending to him, the doctor kept bending over his bed, but the tiny nurselet, almost a little girl, who had summoned up enough strength to heave that electric cannon over from the other room, that angel was already pulling the unneeded machine off against the wall. I realized that the patient had been saved.

I am ashamed to mention it, but at that moment some sort of blasted sob came from my throat. I turned my head away so they wouldn't see how moved I was. But they were busy about their affairs. Relaxed, joking, they returned to the monitoring enclosure. Behind the pane I saw their smiling faces; the doctor had put his hands back into his pockets, as if nothing had happened, although from time to time he stole a look at the monitor.

And I cried. I dissolved in tears like an old woman as I gazed at a bar of sunlight on the opposite wall. The last time I cried like that had been in childhood. I had seen many dreadful things in my life, a good deal of tragedy and death. But this was the first time I had witnessed resurrection. For the first time a man had died in my presence, and others had drawn him back from heaven to earth.

I have seen works of genius in film, I have sat through extraordinary theater performances, I have gazed at all the wonders of the world, but that fraction of a minute in a Warsaw hospital was the most staggering spectacle of all, and the most magnificent I shall ever experience.

During his rounds the next day, a medical professor halted by the mechanic's bed. "How much did you knock back day before yesterday?" he asked the patient. "Half a quart? A whole quart?"

The mechanic, or was he a smith, was suddenly abashed. "Nah—that's way off. Half a quart, the three of us."

The professor nodded understandingly.

"Doctor," the patient said in an irresolute tone. "How many days till I get out? The thing is, I have a woman waiting for me, my fiancée, you might say. I'm going to get married."

The professor smiled an evasive smile. "You'd better not think of marriage for the time being. We have to get a little better first."

The mechanic or blacksmith squinted at this, not overly satisfied with the course of the conversation. He did not know that he had been on the yonder side and had returned to us. Even if they were to tell him about it he would not believe it. Unwittingly he had already been where one awaits the Last Judgment, and unwittingly he had made the leap back into the chill fires of our hell.

Ambition

My ambition is the bane of my life. My ambition is a horrible ogre lodged inside me. My ambition is an onerous burden which I carry to a goal I cannot reach. What goal? That's just it, I don't know.

This monstrously overgrown, morbid ambition would be nothing bad if it were not for the awful disproportion between my ambition and my capabilities, my ability to position myself properly among the omnivorous mammals, my talent for securing esteem, even homage from the other members of the tribe. In a word, there blazes in me an infernal ambition, not to be slaked by the slender stream of my talents, which trickle ever more thinly and feebly.

My towering ambition, worthy of a dinosaur rather than a small mammal, and its symbiosis with those microscopic abilities are only half the trouble. What is worse is that this unpleasant malady produces additional repulsive side effects: a wildly luxuriating shyness and a daily and perpetually swelling, bulging, dilating, tumescent pride, which is beginning to be a pain even to myself.

There was a time when things were very different. When everything was lofty, pure, noble. Observing my neighbors' misshapen lives, I used to wonder why they were unable to return to the path of simplicity, although it was so easy. Why they didn't want to live lives of dignity, beauty, and reason, although it cost so little.

I had already planned my future life neatly at that point. During sleepless nights, on dull Sunday afternoons, and in those low hours one somehow has to wait out, I laid out the shape of the fate awaiting me. I molded it in my imagination so as to avoid philistinism, pettiness, posturing, greed, zealotry, vainglory, envy, and a dozen other vices that turn our short life into hell. But later it turned out that my ambition to live life in a manner aesthetically superior to that of my fellows proved vain. I fared like the others: now comically, now miserably, now up on a crest, now deep down in a ditch, at times beautifully, but most often nastily.

To make up for this, ambition produced damnable side effects. Let us first examine shyness. Mother of God, what have I not suffered through shyness! Everything embarrasses me. I am ashamed to call attention to myself, I am ashamed to ask for directions in the street, I am ashamed to groan when the doctor rips my belly open, I am ashamed to walk into a shop and buy a loaf of bread, I am ashamed to stroll down the street with my wife or to enter the stairwell where my girlfriend lives; I am ashamed of coming from a poor family, I am ashamed to step into an office, ashamed to go to confession; I am ashamed to be a nobody, but would also be ashamed to be President. I am ashamed from morning to evening, even at night, in my sleep. My dreams, hallucinations, nightmares are bashful. Shame drags after me like a train, and shame runs ahead of me like an unmuzzled dog. I flounder through life in a cloud of shame. I sound like shame, I sting with shame, I stink of shame.

And now about pride. That dreadful gland you cannot get the better of, which constantly exudes an awful, repulsive substance that poisons the entire organism. This pride grows along with me; that is, it was small when I was small, and now it is big because I am big. I have stopped growing, but it keeps on. It now keeps pace with my years. The more years, the more pride. You know that moment when a person suddenly tells himself: If they don't respect me, I'll have to respect myself. You recall those violent outbursts of rage if somebody passes you over or fails to appreciate you fully.

That ghastly pride will suddenly dry up in a matter of minutes from causes unknown. Then I go into a panic, keenly feel my nothingness, hear myself like an empty barrel, see the squalor of my unnecessary existence; at such a moment I feel like vanishing, disappearing from the face of the earth, collapsing into intergalactic space. And as I wallow like that in self-denigration, a tall wave of pride returns from somewhere. It floods me, lifts me up, smothers me in whipped-up foam. I begin to look down upon that mediocrity around me, the dumb rabble, the worthless rivals. I feel contempt and preen myself. Preen myself and feel contempt. I am on a high by now and look at everything from above.

Ambition drives me through the deserts and steppes of this world. Ambition chases all of you, my dear rivals. Even if you put on Lord knows what airs of nonchalance, even if you swear a thousand times that you don't care about anything, were you even to stretch a hand out from the grave in a gesture of humility and self-abasement, I still would not believe you, I, your brother, the patient in the neighboring bed who suffers from the same disease, the essence of which is the lust for self-aggrandizement, lording it over one's neighbors, unacknowledged self-deification.

Loneliness

This morning Danka, my wife, took a plane to America. Today, meaning on May 1. We had trouble plowing our way through the jammed city to the airport. Three hours before the scheduled departure we were already moving along a cordoned lane marked by ropes as thick as steamer cables; we were walking this lane in the airport hall and thanking the Lord for our own foresight. You could bet that at check-in time there would turn up a crowd, a mob, a Tatar horde of travelers from all over Poland, groaning under the load of suitcases, chests, packs. This airport is well prepared for its duties. Once you enter this enfencement of ropes, you don't get out of it again, and you end up where you need to.

The city now is as if under siege. Barriers, squads, patrols. The whole city center impassable, armored water cannon here and there, strings of police vehicles showing in their grilled windows cheerful young faces, glinting visored helmets, and the outlines of Japanese plastic shields.

May 1 under special surveillance. A demonstration of laboring folk, of the entire populace of Warsaw, under the protection of armored cars and battalions of people's police. At this point Mr. Censor's pencil descends upon my knockkneed syllables and starts cutting. But please hold your horses, my unknown attentive reader, my companion for close to forty years. Consider, please, that I myself, voluntarily, insert my manuscript into that mysterious machine whence it later issues emaciated, gap-toothed, and deballed. Your crotchety ways have even made me take up self-censorship. And I have, after all, been doing this to myself, with a brief interruption, for several decades. So please put away that pencil, black or red. I say as much as is necessary; and it is better that I should say it than some raging, obsessive whippersnapper.

You cannot hide the fact, then, however badly you may want to, that this workers' holiday takes place under special surveillance, and it looks as if the demonstrators are being guarded against themselves. I mention this in passing, for local color, in deference to certain epic rules. And here I suddenly remember that for many years I, too, used to walk in these parades. Ten years, perhaps, or fifteen. Some years I joined in order to avoid difficulties, though pretending to go voluntarily; other times I really went unforced, from habit, in order to meet colleagues, to sit in the sun surrounded by that unique hullabaloo of band music, metallic slogans from microphones, choruses, and the ceaseless stamping of hundreds of thousands of human feet. May 1 is not a native feast day of mine. Shameful to admit, in Wilno or, rather, near Wilno where I lived, May 1 was never even mentioned. The city may have held parades, I may have been notified of the fact at some point at some meeting, but at the time, before the war, May 1 was an ordinary day to my family and those I associated with.

After the war, though, I went many times. For some time, the parade used to disband on the overpass of Poniatowski Bridge. And in one of the houses under the overpass lived my brother-in-law, Janek Lenica. I remember how one year after the parade a whole flock of us, lobster-red with sunburn and completely worn out, dropped in on Janek to have a drink. And Janek came through with some pretty high-quality stuff, perhaps even of imperialist origin. We drank on an empty stomach. Need I say more? Misery ensued . . .

I remember our return trip. I was lugging Zosia, the wife of my friend the whimsical poet Krzyś, who streaked ahead of us out of embarrassment. I, for my sins, had to schlepp his wife, the gravely inebriated Zosia, actually carrying her on my shoulders amid the colorful streams of demonstrators, who were generous with their remarks, comments, and profound reflections. Nowadays drunks evoke compassion and an indulgent smile, but back then they were still denounced. So I crawled in a state of disgrace, tormented by the whistles and roars of the gaping rabble, dear little Zosia on my back, down Princes Street to Three Crosses Square, which was the stand of a number of taxis run by cabbies with mugs purple from overindulgence, where I expected to find understanding and fraternal assistance.

But why do I recall that sunny spring of many, many years ago? There is no Zosia anymore, there is no Krzyś. That is, they exist, but they live far away, separated from me by seven rivers and seven mountains; they are alive and I am alive, although at one time it seemed that we couldn't live without each other.

And now I am alone. Alone with the cat Ivan. Alone in the back yard of New World Avenue. Danka has flown to the other world, to America, that is. The cat sensed this calamity. Since yesterday he has been offended, hostile, uncouth. He thought we were both going, leaving him at the mercy of fate. But when I came home from the airport he ran up to me and told me a long story. I don't understand all that the cat Ivan tells me. I take it he spoke of his fears and of his joy when they proved groundless. Right now he is lying under the radiator, which is still heated although it is May, lying on his side and diligently washing the costly fur on his belly and hindquarters.

I really meant to whine about my loneliness, you know. Quite against my intention I got sidetracked to that May Day which may irritate Mr. Censor. I meant to draft a little essay about human loneliness in a big city. But halfway there the idea went up in smoke, faded and turned to frowst: Lord, how many such little essays I have read in my time!

I am a herd animal. I need co-workers, an audience, a crowd. This isn't because I am gregarious, though, for fundamentally I am not at all. I need noise, murmur, hubbub around me. Monotonous and prolonged sounds which set my brain whorls vibrating, thus keeping the gray matter that fills my skull from its own autonomous chemical processes, which urge me toward madness.

But my most beloved friend, the actor Gucio H. (I omit his name, and shall never cite names anymore, I run into enough unpleasantness as it is), well, this Gucio one day, telling about a certain colleague who lost his mind all of a sudden, gave me a look and said: "But you, Tadzio, will never go crazy."

This was a comfort, but at the same time an impertinence. A comfort in that I would avoid a sinister fate and horrid misfortunes; an impertinence because today's artists, operating in the art biz, alert, organized, possessed of a highly developed accountancy, are afraid of sobriety and normality. They know that art feeds on insanity, and so at times they even simulate derangement and search—as a sick animal seeks healing greens—for fool's parsley, wolfberries, or swallowwort.

Loneliness in a state of fever. The fever of a sick country. My country is unhealthy, but then, the whole world is sick. And I have a bunch of years ahead of me. A certain kind palmist prophesied for me a fearfully long life. She showed me my Lifeline on my palm. It was endless, a virtually unending line, for it ran from the inside of the hand to the top and took off across fingers and fingernails into the blue yonder, to some point of infinity—which I don't want or need to have any use for.

The sun is shining—the ball of flaming gases we could not live without for even a minute. Ivan is asleep by now under the radiator. I flounder about among my usual trains of thought, couched in my usual stylistics. On the rim of New World Avenue, which in spite of everything is not my world.

Frights of Spring

Spring has come. A caricature of spring. Weird, sickly, not quite springlike. And above all—drought. Water is becoming an ever greater problem. Water runs off, disappears. Becomes extinct like wild animals. Water is the first to be wiped out.

You may say that we have destroyed our native environment. However, it surely wasn't me who contributed to this. Quite the reverse: for nearly twenty years I have been crying woe over its slow but ever accelerating demise.

I remember Julian Przyboś, the poet, in his review of *Ascension* falling with particular fury upon my apostrophes to moribund nature. Like a somewhat displaced Futurist, he poured scorn on my hayseed sentimentalism, my oafish attachment to rusticity, my dull-witted and reactionary hostility to progress.

Yes—those Futurists, modernists, or whatever, went into raptures over cities of ferroconcrete. That was the new beauty, the progressives' aesthetic, the canon of the future.

But less than forty years went by, not even half a century, and it turned out that they were left far behind, in a fearful backwardness, totally outdated. Yes indeed, perhaps they fulfilled some sort of provisional destiny of their own as bards of urbanization and industrial advance. But presently, almost instantly, they became figures of the past.

The old poet made fun of those appeals in defense of woods, rivers, skies, because he didn't know, didn't guess, never noticed that the rivers were dead, the woods drying, the skies covered by a perpetual haze of garbage.

Yes—but that was long ago. It is over, we have forgotten about those delusions and errors, a new spring is at hand, such as it is: exiguous, elderly somehow, rather unconvincing, but in this spavined condition, available to all; democratic as can be.

But where we are, in the gorges, ravines, and glens of New World Avenue, drug addicts have made their appearance. Their domicile, their native land, perhaps even in a pathetic sense their empire, is Tuwim Street, named for the poet to whom I used to deliver the proofs of *Rebirth*, for which he wrote a little satirical column called "Camera Obscura." And today the lane that bears his name boils over with young junkies. The cellars and stairwells of our apartment house are their real citadel. When I step out on the stairs in the morning I see traces of their presence—vials and flasks of sorts and streaks of blackened blood all over a wall, right up to the ceiling, where somebody evidently hit a vein the wrong way.

Once—it must have been in late autumn—I saw one of them being carried out of the basement. Two ambulance medics set down the stretcher in the middle of the courtyard. On the stretcher lay a bearded young man of the sort you see in their millions in the streets, railroad stations, movie theaters, offices, churches. There he lay with his arms crossed over his chest in the light autumn drizzle that had been coming down since morning, lay unmoving in a coarse homemade gray sweater, and must have been dead by then, for two policemen were unhurriedly picking over his green backpack containing the modest effects of a wanderer who with a "country music" song on his pale lips imitates someone heard on the radio or seen in a flick.

So he lay dead on that nasty autumn day, and no one among the inhabitants of our building showed any interest. Only I stopped beside the stretcher, looked at the damp matted hair and upturned Jesus beard, and thought of all those young people and of myself. And in that brief interval I thought of the stubborn search for new ways of stifling oneself, protesting against a stupid and unwanted existence, and committing suicide without laying violent hands on that shitty life.

From somewhere they flock together like birds. Some elegantly and fashionably dressed, with the presence of graduates of elite private schools, but others more like twisted draggletails bearing the stamp of degeneracy on their faces. They divide into groups of ten to twenty members, pull out little wallets, sell something, buy something, then vanish into those ill-starred stairwells; and after that, shivering, staggering, supported by those still somewhat more conscious among them, they scatter to their everyday lives, and only their field surgeons, those dispatchers into the lands of oblivion, those marginally together ones, turn on a street hydrant and rinse out the white plastic syringes in the water jet.

Sometimes I am seized by the typical rage of the embittered old man. In our time, let me tell you, this kind of lawlessness would have been unthinkable. We, let me tell you, worked hard for a living, we fought for our country's freedom, yes sir, not sparing our blood. And here, sir, these freeloaders . . . and so on and so forth. But I am sensible, after all; I know that you have to measure the present day with today's measure. And so I watch these young bedraggled dandies and sophisticated hoboes who stray vacant-eyed around New World Avenue, living corpses, dead survivors, with one leg here in the old New World, the other in a new one. I pity them, my heart aches for them, yet on the other side, somewhere, there is something like a twinge of jealousy, a tiny yen to have a go at it myself.

You philosophers, what does it all mean? What does nature have in mind, or Providence, or perhaps just the lowly "logic of history"? They are doing what they want, after all. Somebody who had been in the Congress Hall at some rock idol's show told me that the entire audience, "sent" by the music, spent the whole concert in copulation. Screwing away as natural as you please on those purple upholstered seats, which remember other times and other historic events. After all, they can choose to work or not to work and be supported by their parents. After all, they can stand against a wall in the street and pee as people pass by. After all, they can go up to a wealthy man and tell him: Let's have your change, brother, we want to be rich, too.

The great paroxysm of democracy which runs through the world, caused very likely by some strange civilizational leap, the gigantic democratic explosion like an earthquake, but a global one, this rehearsal of the end of the world has not yielded any relief. Everyone is still unhappier than in the times of slavery, feudalism, or the horrible era of early capitalism. Not unhappier, perhaps, but equally unhappy.

Why does an equal or nearly equal share in our joint existence increase general and individual desperation? Why do all the promises of the philosophers, sages, and theoreticians of the past seem to be turning on their heads? Why don't they taste to us as they should? Why doesn't the world become happier, although it should?

Here I am, posing rhetorical questions to myself, to which no one has answers, after all, and even if they do, I don't want to listen to them. For this epoch of general, worldwide democratization is also the era of the know-it-alls. Pestilential pullulating wiseacres.

An American friend of ours, Joanna, who had visited Poland, wrote us a card after her return to the States: "Everybody here asks about everything, but nobody listens to the answers."

Schlemieldom

First heat wave of the year. Premature, unnecessary swelter. A bit of unrest in town, spot of mild tension. Water cannon and police cars drawn up in the alleys. Familiar genre pictures of Warsaw. Been like this for a few years now.

But what I am thinking of is the old no-go or mess-up. Not hard luck, but failure. No-go is what the majority of people suffer from. There are lucky dogs for whom everything comes up roses. Whatever they touch turns to gold. Let them even stumble in the street and come a cropper, and they'll stumble on a wallet stuffed with bills that some rich fellow has lost.

This brings me to the question of where the lucky dogs come from—and I have known a lot of them in my time. Many, of course, helped their good fortune along; others did little and still lucked out. I have a notion that the mathematics of large numbers has something to do with it, game theory or something along that line that I once heard from Professor Steinhaus. But I probably muddled it up; it doesn't matter, the point is that sometimes on the roulette wheel the same number comes up a dozen times or more. So among people, too, there'll be lucky numbers for whom everything works out many years in a row.

I don't believe in luck being the finger of God. I believe in luck as a happy accident, a favorable combination of circumstances, the simple upshot of mathematics.

But what do I care about lucky dogs. Let's return to schlemieldom, which is closer to me, which I have been communing with from childhood on, to which I have allied myself for life.

Everybody looks himself over like a racehorse at the starting gate. I don't actually know whether racehorses look themselves over, but they ought to. And so, looking myself over for years, I have noticed certain regularities in my fate. What I find is that in the larger view I have been lucky, sort of. I came out unscathed from several tyrannies, my subsequent life, too, did not work out too badly, there were even episodes of what you could call success. Altogether, in the eyes of my colleagues the course of my life probably looks like one broad band of happiness.

Yet I know well that it is a washout. Not a case of bad luck, not an egregious flop or failure or outright disaster, but an ordinary, low-visibility, inconspicuous, almost transparent washout. Something, you see, would begin to go right for me, when suddenly, all at once, it stopped going or died a slow death. Some other time my line might jerk, as it were, I'd start reeling in, some enticing perspectives would outline themselves, and abruptly, for no reason you could see, begin to fade, blanch, melt into nothingness. My "go" is the puniest little ember, exposed to the rain and the icy winds. It glimmers and dies down, hisses and flickers up in a small flame, but presently is smothered in smoke. The little flame will rise, you see, creep over on some kindling, begin to turn into a fire, but suddenly give a quiver, shrink, die down, shyly show its face once more from below, quake, shiver, shoot up sparks, and be gone.

I used to like my schlemieldom. It was close and dear to me, like a crippled child. Though a handicap, it was of service to me. It mobilized me, stirred me to battle, imbued me with ferocity and an undefined craving for vengeance.

It always took the form of some juicy kicks from a solicitous destiny, some unexpected blows from bored Providence, abrupt insults from the heavenly powers, if there are such, and if they take an interest in me. It was those blows and licks that egged me on, as a lazy horse is goaded by the spur, and I would rouse myself to a brisker trot and drag my wagon of sins, impediments, and incapacities at a livelier pace.

I really cherished those tribulations of mine. I cherished those states of stinging chagrin in which I dragged myself home, lay down on the couch with my face to the wall, and tried to fight down the ache, the disgust, the tumult of harsh thoughts and grievous feelings in my heart. This done, I would get up and go to work—if what I do may be called work.

For some time, though, starting in the recent past, actually, schlemieldom has ceased being lucrative, has become unprofitable. At present my quality is an ordinary rotten schlemielhood which robs one of the zest for living, paralyzes the internal energies, and kills one's self-confidence.

Something to the point. In the sixties in the Warsaw Guard there was a fighter, a heavyweight, who either won his fights by a knockout or lost them by a knockout. I have always had the feeling that I was his spiritual brother. I have always felt when I took pen in hand that I was one step away from a knockout.

Providence has denied me professional status in my discipline. For almost forty years now I have been an amateur in the literary métier. When I start writing I never know where it is going to take me—uphill or downhill or, rather, into the gulch of graphomania. I have never been able to tell myself, as others do: Now then, I am starting a book, and in fourteen months' time I will finish it, publish it, gather in praises and critical remarks, and put it on the shelf among my other books, which are my manifest achievement.

I fly but don't know when I'll fall. I levitate but don't know when I may flop into trashiness. I dispute with the Lord but don't know when I'll feel His fist between my eyes.

I am an amateur, and I have constructed a set of premises to fit this status. I want to be fresh, sincere, spontaneous, uninhibited, natural, genuine, unaffected, free from routines and professional prejudices, without all those ludicrous features which are the risks of a chancy occupation. I am an amateur—one who has avoided the pitfalls of professionalism but who has fallen into the wolf trap of incompetence instead.

Now it is my turn to meet my fate. And I am reminded of Jerzy Andrzejewski, my elder brother, who has probably turned to dust by now, my elder brother in the tussle with life, which

my mother as a young woman

every moment changes shape, color, consistency in our hands. Jerzy comes to my mind from time to time because he was practically a textbook specimen of the Polish literary man, whose example will most readily enable us to trace the high flights and the falls, the graces and blemishes, pains and glories of our contemporary literature.

But I've been sidetracked for a while, following a colleague who is gone forever. Yet my concern is my schlemieldom after all, which is not of such outstanding importance. Of no importance, in fact; but for me it is.

I even know how I could save myself. Many of my readers, genuine or bogus, have suggested to me a return to narrative prose, tried to talk me into a normal plot with normal descriptions of nature, encouraged me to write novels as ordained by Our Lord, without unhealthy ambitions, excessive pretensions, a provincial's urge to innovate. I said that I am being urged to resume writing novels, but did I actually know how to do that?

For there was a time when I was tempted to try to take the measure of prose as it was written a hundred years ago: solid, sterling, at once instructive and entertaining. What came of this was my *Power*.

I would honestly prefer to crush rock on a highway, though, than to write standard, regular novels. Those novels revolt me like carrion. And even if I made myself sit down and start grinding away at this feudal toil which is so dear to readers good and bad, smart and dull, naïve and sophisticated, and even if I did violence to myself, my hands would refuse to serve me, and all of a sudden my heart would burst. The heart of a genuine amateur—an involuntary amateur. Amateur for lack of that inner greatness which is the result of chemistry rubbing against electricity—or a sign from God.

Excursion to Cracow

All I meant to say was that now, today, at this moment, at the fag end of life, schlemieldom weakens me, smothers my élan, kills my belief in myself. I am as timid as a rabbit. When I reach for the pen of my former friend, the cameraman of several of my films, when I reach for that pen, when I take from the drawer the old paper already used by somebody on one side, in the course of these preliminaries my heart pounds against my ribs, my hands shake, and I feel the kind of choking sensation I felt in the dim past when I was learning the difficult art of love, when for the first time in my life I embraced a woman and to the thunder of bells in my head tried to make her mine.

Hardly have I written a few pages when later at night, actually toward morning, I wake up and, as I wait for daybreak, run over those pages in my mind and compare them with this miserable world around me, that human wretchedness about me, and become keenly conscious of my beggarly state, and realize that I shall never attain even this wretchedness, will be no match for it, not up to it, won't rise a fraction of an inch above its level.

At night I am seized by panic—a strange, idiotic fear of failure. They are delivering the milk, containers banging against the sidewalk; somewhere a cat yowls as if it were being skinned, while I lie there shaking with fear. For some years I have watched my star, and myself, slowly wane. I never expected anything from life, but now it is a hard and painful thing to slide down a moderate slope into the dark trench of oblivion. I didn't expect anything from life, but back then there was health, there were sudden silly onrushes of optimism, and somewhere on the horizon there sometimes glinted perverse hope, deceptively shimmering like the will-o'-the-wisp of my Wilno country. For that matter, in those days ideas fairly pulsated, flared, swelled within me, among them the one which deadens our feelings and sends us into a blind stampede like animals and pushes us headlong to gratification and appeasement, to a second of happiness and a crumb of poetry.

That's what I meant to talk about, but at some point I got sidetracked, carried off into some jumble of thoughts unfinished and sentences broken off halfway. I am doomed to be the kind of person I am.

A storm has gathered. You hear the first shy peals of spring thunder. It has turned dark, like the dark before daybreak, when I am racked by terror over my misspent life. Fat raindrops are drumming on the tin-covered sill. The cat Ivan has sought shelter from the storm.

I sometimes think of Cracow, and now suddenly Cracow came to my mind, the city where I spent almost two years, between 1945 and 1947. I was nineteen and twenty years old then, right in that outstandingly receptive and dynamic period of life. Yet Cracow left no lasting trace on me. That is, it stayed in my imagination as part of a garland of sunny images fragrant with acacias, fresh milk, and simmering stonework, but it didn't settle in my mind to the point where I would have to return to it, where it would enter my dreams or help me in my work, if what I do may be called work. That is why I was unable to give any of my books an authentic Cracow setting. All of them when held up against Cracow instantly began to lose color, smell, movement—in fact, life. Traces of such endeavors may be found in *From a City under Siege* or *Nothing or Nothing*. And that was it.

Yet that city is in me, after all. More so perhaps than Warsaw. But too much in a sentimental and static way, I daresay, conceived too exclusively in aesthetic terms.

An episode as if from an early color movie. (The old movies in color were quite different from those of today, more artificial, saccharine, false.) From that episode I carried away a doleful reflex memory: On Krakowskie Przedmieście, rue Faubourg de Cracovie, I come across a blowsy old tramp, completely white-haired, waddling along with bundles wrapped in newsprint hung all over him, dressed for all kinds of weather regardless of the season; that is to say, in some sort of unspeakably filthy overcoat trussed up with twine, and with a bizarre little cap on his head. He is my former classmate, from the university in Cracow, from Professor Pigon's rooming house. I first met him and got to know him on Krakowskie Przedmieście some twenty years ago. He was still normal, still looked like a teaching assistant of some totally superfluous academic program—although even then you could discern the first signs of a fixation, if not outright derangement. And subsequently, throughout those years that slipped so swiftly into oblivion, he gradually went to seed, decayed physically, became eccentric, and ended up fully qualified for the contingent of Warsaw bums.

I for my part lived in Pigon's rooming house with two fellow students I often think about; and perhaps they may on occasion mention me to their grandchildren. One of them was Wiesio, handsome, cheerful, high-spirited. The other was Roman, sandy-haired, intelligent, with a caustic sense of humor. They were both law students and both came from Dynów, a little town on the San River. Those two years in our digs were completely dominated by the watchword "UPA," the Ukrainian Partisan Movement, which was forever assaulting Dynów or retreating from the vicinity. My roommates were totally engrossed in that feral record of murder, arson, and rapine.

But we were terribly young, after all. Cracow, undestroyed by the war, was a vision from the silver screen. From a prewar color film. And we, meekly and cautiously, nosed about this city, which was big to us—or perhaps just to myself—as though roaming an empire of letters or film. Everybody was hard up, and they had to cram a lot, crawling under their blankets and monotonously reciting entire handbooks of law—although that law was broken constantly and everywhere in the world.

With a certain bemusement I come to realize how very lonely I was then; despite those few colleagues, despite the work in the editorial offices of *Rebirth*, despite the stray lot of people from Wilno who had turned up there, I was fearfully lonesome, completely on my own.

And even that Cracovian love of mine, that unconsummated affair set beneath the chill vaults of the Department of Polish Philology, even that timid rapture was lonesome, forlorn; and I feel sure that the girl involved, with the student cap on her fair head, only once in a blue moon thinks back to that time in Cracow. Perhaps a sort of mirage will stir in her memory when she comes across my mud-bespattered name in a newspaper or hears a casually distorted version of it on the radio.

Mother of God, how I yearned for love in those days. Day and night I panted with gaping jaws. How much emotion, energy, raw strength were burned up in me! If only she had been aware of it, had put two and two together, had sent me a glance with that little smile which I see to this day, although forty strange years have passed by now.

I lived in the Pigon rooming house, and throughout those two years the sun shone, just as it does in the Wilno country. I mean to say that I don't remember any rains or snowstorms in Cracow. Instead, I remember the taste of Italian ices, which could be had everywhere, and the smell, or better, the repulsive subtle stench of the bedbugs which reigned in our digs, lorded it over us, tormented us, and at last ate us alive.

That Cracow sped by me on wings and will never be caught up with again. And I am not going to chase it now, for I was really after something else when I started digressing and tracked down that digression with gusto. But before I took a wrong turn I intended to mention that I have grown tired of my supernatural proclivities, metaphysical leanings, tolerance for superstitions, snobbish interest in charlatans and the haunted. I have stopped gazing at the sky. I don't wait for visitors from space anymore.

The Miracle

I have noticed an arresting phenomenon, which is possibly healthy, possibly morbid in character. It is that older people are beginning to write verse. They have never concerned themselves with poetry before, they have been writing novels, plays, or essays, but today they compose verses.

There is nothing fortuitous about this. There is something that makes people who used to be ashamed of poetry, even of the suspicion of writing poetry, shamelessly write verses and narrative poems and shamelessly publish them in weeklies or monthlies, wherever they have a chance.

Why does the old generation write verse? Why does the young generation fail to? I mean they do, but measured by the above strange disproportion, they seem to write less of it, as if they were leaving the field to the manic old men.

They are manic all right, although their mania is modest in scale, as befits old age. Polish oldsters write verse—though foreign ones do, too, for all I know. But the Polish ones surely find their outlet and fulfillment in poetry, one can see that with the naked eye. I, too, have written some verse, unaware that I had succumbed to a general epidemic. But I am enough of a grizzled old crow to have gone about it cautiously, hiding the senile experiment in a novel and saddling the poor hero of my monotonous prose with the responsibility for my graphomanic excess.

Why do old men write verse? It must be the time we live in. The time is such that it cannot be subsumed in novels anymore, condensed in drama, or screamed about in the press. The time is that way, this is how it rose out of the kneading trough like a crazily puffed-up dough that you have to bite into with verse. Verse is the crying of children and the weeping of old men. Old people in the grip of despair write verse. It is by verse that the old protest against the absence of logic, the crumbling of weights and measures, the victorious entropy that runs amok above us, beneath us, about us. The old men drool in rhyme or without rhyme because they can neither live on nor die in peace.

But what do I have to do with old men who write little poems like young ladies in finishing schools? What is just coming to mind is my immersion in the countryside around Suwałki three years ago. That was the region, at the border of Lithuania and the margin of Belorussia, and leaning ever so lightly on some hamlets of Old Believers, where I made the film *The Issa Valley*. And that Suwałki country quaked under my feet, flamed at night with some glow over the skyline; there was always some vibration in the air, straying waves or native emanations.

Drilling derricks stand out against the sky. They root about in this old earth—the matrix, ages ago, of the princely Jadźwings—they uncover some ores, some treasures. They say that when airplanes fly over this country, their clocks and meters go awry; and that people fall ill more than elsewhere, and always have.

I did feel a certain magic aura around me during the months I lived there at the foot of a windswept mountain on the shores of five lakes. I thought this magic would serve my purposes, would bless my labor, would bring some sudden unexpected happiness. But I had a wretched time. Sorcery wrought its madness around me, witches soared straddling brooms, werewolves howled on the moors, devils knocked at my windows with their fists at night, but on the celluloid tape all remained steady and bland.

Until all of a sudden fate made a gesture in our direction, a really enticing one. On a certain Sunday I was riding in a taxi with the cameraman, Jurek Łukaszewicz, another fellow who licks his chops for miracles. We were tooling along in a sour mood, endlessly dissatisfied with ourselves, still uncertain of our work and our intentions, when suddenly the cabby pipes up to tell us of a local sensation, the big neighborhood hit: at Olecko, not far from here, there has been a miracle. Blood running from a cross.

Jurek and I exchange a quick look, and I tell the driver: "We'll go look at the miracle." "What about the locations?" he asks. "Some other time. Now for Olecko, posthaste."

Now, this little town, which competed unsuccessfully with Suwałki for the status of provincial capital, this Olecko, this tidy German hamlet on a tidy lake, had an instantly recognizable topography—here was the high school, there the county courthouse, there the sports arena, there a good restaurant with fish on the menu. And if I didn't walk in fear of Mr. Censor, I would even venture to assert that these two neighboring little towns accurately represent two neighboring continents. Olecko is a small-scale replica of the attainments of Europe, while Suwałki proudly exhibits all the virtues of Asiatic civilization.

So we speed with pulses racing to Olecko, cross the little town with its large red-brick buildings, and pull up to the church, which is uninteresting, ordinary, without signs of antiquity. All over the front yard of the church there was a throng of people kneeling, standing, or milling about a tall wooden cross painted a kind of muddy oil color, not exactly brown, not quite gray— in a word, the color provincials use to paint front doors, jambs, or the banisters of attic stairs. Through the interstices between praying figures we can make out burning candles and stacks of flowers.

Let's film the miracle, I tell my team. We only have to go about it discreetly. Jurek nods, he has a talent for getting along with people anyway, people never do him any harm. We quietly get our gear out. But people begin to turn around and inspect us; we have a bit of a Warsaw look about us, something governmental or at least official.

Still, the risk is worth taking. We get to see something of the miracle. Near where the arms of the cross meet the upright, a dark substance oozes from the cracks and runs down the trunk. I walk all around the cross. From all sides something trickles, something dark, colorless, not at all like bleeding, yet possibly congealed, blackened blood.

I seek out the parish priest and ask permission for our sacrilegious filming. The priest, rather nonplussed himself, gives his permission. He is cautious and skeptical in advance regarding the possibility of a miracle. There is some flow, certainly, although the cross is old. But some time ago it was treated with a preservative. On the other hand, the laboratory which was commissioned to perform an analysis of the fluid found that it had characteristics of human blood. For the time being nothing was known for sure; but news of the miracle was spreading with lightning speed, thousands of people were worshipping the wondrous cross day and night, and nobody could tell what might come of it all.

But we know what we need. We set up our gear and shoot away, now here, now there, now from this, now from that angle, not sparing our supply of film, which is on the meager side. Sunshine flickers through the branches of trees. Silence reigns round about, only occasionally broken by a timid whisper. This crowd walks on tiptoe. This crowd holds its breath. This crowd awaits a divine blessing which will change the plight of individuals and of the country as a whole.

We have recorded on chemically treated tape the banal lines of the German church, and the great heft of the ordinary, commonplace cross done up in oil paint like a garden bench, and people's faces, common human faces thirsting for holiness.

This is not a showy, colorful, bombastic miracle. It is a homespun, provincial, meager one, like all this countryside and these people who are kneeling on the damp gravel with their weathered and badly toilworn hands piously folded.

We left that place torn by baffling emotions. Was that wonder perpetuated on our roll of film, or did it leave the film untouched by virtue of its miraculous quality? Or would one perhaps find exposed in rainbow blazes an apotheosis of divine power, contained in unusual signs and commands which would change the course of things on our earth or, at the least, endow us gray bread eaters with a pinch of illusory freedom, a freedom as humble as an overcast day redolent with the perfumes of a still distant spring.

But the darkroom yielded a film with exposures like those of any location shoot. What was immortalized on celluloid tape was only what we had seen ourselves, nothing more. Yet I decided to tack those snatches of provincial views onto a film about a different time and different people. Just for luck. Just to soothe a kind of metaphysical disquiet that preyed on me and my friends. Like a prayer whispered on the road. Like an Angel of the Lord at the parting of the ways.

It happened, and it passed. It sank into the gloom of oblivion. Without an echo. Nobody ever mentioned the miracle of Olecko later on. Other miracles came to pass.

But I actually had something else in mind, as usual. For I had again changed a little in the course of the last few years. As recently as ten years ago I scorned common sense, made fun of nineteenth-century rationalism, gave the persecutors of quacks and wise women a very hard time. Until I had to be admonished in one of his last columns by Antoni Słonimski, the ever lamented, forever dear to me. And he did this so discreetly, so gently and privately, that only I understood to whom the caution was addressed. And this missive from Antoni lodged in me several years; this testament of the last nineteenth-century rationalist and liberal stuck in the pocket over my heart, that attentive gaze of a dead friend accompanied the rough and the smooth of my fate. Until one day I at last realized with astonishment that I had stopped waiting for extraterrestrials, that I had lost interest in voyages by UFOs, that I was a little annoyed by all those wonder-workers, possessed, and holy fools.

Common sense is often harmful, but lunacy is no solution either. In general one tires of life. Yet one has to live, after all, since there is no other alternative. My dear palmist, Bieta, has prophesied me many more years of life; and two years from now, she predicted, there would be some sort of powerful intellectual explosion in my biography. But two years from now I'll be sixty. All-holiest Mother of God, sixty years old. What intellectual outburst can still threaten me? Surely nothing but an ordinary brain hemorrhage. O merciful God.

Portrait of a Short Short-Story Writer

The prose that comes out of my typewriter is dismal. Yet haven't I always been known as a literary ladies' man in the salons of

Warsaw, cock of the walk, Merry-Andy? I don't want to praise myself, but when all is said and done, for the sake of the truth (quite a stylistic flourish, that), in order not to lie, I have to drop the perfunctory remark that one evening at a party I was so brilliantly witty that as a result of a sally of mine a certain eminent critic and publicist let go what is known as a bubble of gas or, more simply, farted with laughter.

So it did occur to me at times to be funny, and many readers expressed their gratitude for the more hilarious pages. Perhaps I am exaggerating a bit, talking of "many," but four or five is the absolute truth. Here, though, I recall with some chagrin the time when over a little vodka a dear colleague and rival of mine in the writing business began to reproach me for being so witty in life yet so totally devoid of humor in my prose. And I listened to him, swallowing bitter spittle and feeling close to tears. For say what you like, I thought, perhaps I am a poor stylist, perhaps my writing lacks depth, perhaps I am a miserable psychologist, but surely there were times when I have amused the reader. And this is my sole comfort, my only reason for composing narrative prose, and who knows, but my sole ultimate merit— and this honest simpleton finds fault with me for lack of humor and encourages me to write more wittily.

In this present hogskin of mine (that is what we used to call books at school) I feel far removed from any humorous vein. "Far from a humorous vein" is not nearly enough: the vein simply does not appear, and I myself have forgotten about it. I think it is the fault of the times. The times are anything but gay, anything but conducive to wit, and devoid of a sense of humor.

But where everything around is on the glum side, it is fitting to bring up Zdzisław Maklakiewicz, actor and friend of many people of different callings, and also my friend, colleague, and collaborator, for we toiled together on two of my films.

Well, this Zdzisio was a poet of delicate humor, dainty wit, sophisticated facetiousness. He belonged to the same species of genius as the famous Franc Fiszer, whom I know only indirectly, from the reports of my older friends. There is a category of genius which cannot be perpetuated in any material way; that is to say, its quality cannot be defined or reproduced in print or sound or even on film. Geniuses of this quality occur once in a generation; they vitalize and exalt us, teach us to comprehend true poetry, and having accomplished this, they remain within us and perish in us forever, or rather perish along with us.

One may well despair, of course, over the fact that their talent resides in part in its very immunity to being arrested in time and converted into negotiable property, the fact that it has the life of a butterfly and resembles an ephemeral cloud pattern in the sky. But what makes their gift one of genius is that it links itself with the moment, with the briefest unit of time, with a sort of joint flare-up of intellect and emotion, something like an abrupt flash of the divine.

And I don't regret in the least that it wasn't possible to record what was greatest about Zdzisio, although we have many of his outstanding roles preserved on film. I mean, perhaps I do regret it, but I don't despair, because I know that that ectoplasm of genius which he gave off in the small hours was bound to die in our frosty, oxygen-poor, toxic air. Our air or any other. For the law governing the birth and death of poetry decrees that it is created by legendary geniuses once in several generations.

We always liked to romance about Zdzisio in his lifetime. By now, some years after his death, he is a venerable legend. One or another of us will really sweat at times trying to re-create a certain scenario, one he was always planning to put on film, the story of a little stick floating along a winding stream—of the adventures of this twig, adventures full of psychological truth, uncommon drama, and subtle charm.

I myself lifted one of Maklakiewicz's minisketches for my book *Nothing or Nothing*—"minisketch" is probably the proper term for the microspectacle involved. Zdzisio, you see, showed us once how in high summer, under a sweltering sun, the tipplers beleaguer the beer concession. They are so thirsty—so ideally will that beer suit them on that sizzling noon—such a near-worship do they feel toward that fluid—that the kiosk turns into a kind of sanctuary, and the blazing vacancy next to it also acquires a magic power. So they lift the open bottles of cold foaming liquid unhurriedly to their lips, tilt their heads back,

our house in the Wilno Colony

half close their eyes, and freeze in the majestic pose of the bugler; and for the first time the Adam's apple twitches with delight, and then, why then a festive flourish of bugles breaks loose like the hourly trumpet call from St. Mary's in Cracow, making it seem as if that little knot of parched sots was producing a cascade of sounds known all over the world. It was the radio playing, of course. The proprietor's transistor radio.

When we were doing films together, Zdzisio would sometimes come up to me and take me to one side. Once there, he would say: Look, old fellow, listen, this is how I am going to act this. Then he acted it out as nobody in the world could have done.

Next, out on location, I'd issue the order: Camera! The machine would go into motion with a low buzz, and Zdzisio would act like a bump on a log, or at best like an ordinary decent actor of the Warsaw stage.

Zdzisio was (God, how disgusting this familiarity of mine is, but I really can't talk about him as Mr. Maklakiewicz, for he was Zdzisio, Zdzisio to everybody, to directors and gofers, to stage managers and drivers, to great ladies and ordinary rubble nymphs)—to resume, Zdzisio was . . . but by this time my digression has made me forget what I meant to say. What I must have had in mind was that Zdzisio was a genius at re-hearsals. At stage or film rehearsals, at rehearsing how to live by the Lord's mercy, or how to tear himself loose for a while from our miserable earth and soar skyward for a short moment, whatever the sky might be like.

Shortly before his death, Zdzisio played an engagement at my New World Avenue; that is, in the Kameralny Theater on nearby Foksal Street. He had some sort of minor role in a performance I don't remember. But about this part of his he had this to tell me later:

"I step on stage, begin my act, and feel I am doing magnifi-cently. I simply grab the audience by the puss and keep them twisting. And after the performance, when I am back out on Foksal Street, suddenly a couple of characters come up to me out of the shadows. 'Was it you,' they ask, 'who grabbed us by the puss in the theater and kept us twisting?' 'Yes, that was me,' I answer. 'Well, so now we are going to grab you by the puss and keep you twisting.' "

Żagary

I have drawn the thick curtains over the windows and decreed night for myself—jumping to eight-thirty although it is barely evening in early spring. This night is clearly on the artificial side; daylight filters through the curtain cloth, or more properly, the afterglow of sunset. The cat Ivan, confounded by my freak-ishness, has taken to hunting in the passage for early, pre-mid-night ghosts, phantoms, and vampires. I can hear his muffled leaps and rather plaintive cries from here.

Not long ago an acquaintance offered me a compliment of a sort on my book *Moonrise, Moonset*. But since this was a scru-pulous person, he did not fail to remark, by way of criticism, that it was an uneven work. Now this chilled me to the marrow of my bones. Well, perhaps I exaggerate a little, not to the marrow—but I did feel a trifle chagrined.

Later I attempted to examine that imputation with all due

seriousness. And it occurred to me, rightly or wrongly, that my interlocutor had in mind a certain heterogeneity in the subject matter of the work. The fact that in it I attempt to talk about matters of ultimate importance to our society as well as about some fairly insignificant colleagues. That as I allow myself to expatiate slightly on my understanding of cosmogony, I also recollect various erotic episodes. That I write about Literature with a capital *L* as well as about the trollops of Warsaw. So that is perhaps what strikes my acquaintance as unevenness. For experience has taught him that if a worthy author starts his book with king and country, then he will march arm in arm with them to the final page. Or if he takes up sex, he will stay with sex.

The point is that I invested considerable effort into making my little screeds, such as *The Calendar and the Hourglass* and that *Moonrise, Moonset*, uneven. I sweated bullets over the loosely tessellated, nonchalant, if you will, construction of these brochures. What I was looking for was farrago, turmoil, cacophony.

For I am the last of the fabulists, storytellers, of the old gentry. Not so long ago there still lived such masters of that Polish literary genre as Wańkowicz, Mackiewicz, or Father Meysztowicz. But they are gone now, those great Polish squires or, more properly, Lithuanian or Belorussian ones. Just recently I read in some contemporary Belorussian monthly a column about an old Belorussian family, the Wańkowiczes. The author notes that one of these Wańkowiczes, Melchior, did a lot of writing in Polish and spent part of his life in Poland. As I said, they aren't about anymore, those old gentlemen of hoary nobility who through the ages occupied the front seats in the senate house of the Polish-Lithuanian Commonwealth, or disdained the episcopal purple.

Perhaps at one time this species occurred in the Polish Crown lands, too; but of late times, within our memory at least, it has been in evidence only in the Wilno province. That is why I— of lowly Wilno squirarchy, descended from humble land-tilling yeomen—subconsciously and instinctively, as it were, at some point in my wretched life took up the art of the yarn, albeit under cover of some kind of diary or memorandum writing. For I had grown up in an atmosphere of storytelling, humorous narrative, and anecdotage of the nobility. Until the Second World War, and actually until the coming of the Bolsheviks, which ushered in a new epoch, people in our sphere lived in the nineteenth century. The evening fabulation over glass, decanter, or pitcher was our newspaper, our calendar, our encyclopedia; it took the place of book, concert, cinema.

Even while I was already here in Warsaw I had occasion to spend time in a house of the Wilno culture, belonging to the famous basso Bernard Ladysz. I was generally asked there to attend some family celebration. And though the house was equipped with every sort of audio-visual apparatus, at a certain moment—an opportune one, to be sure—Mama Ladysz would intone a song that used to be sung in the old home in the Wilno country, and all picked up the beautiful tune; but Benka was by no means the first in this chorus, Mama Ladysz even took him to task a bit when he sharped or flatted. The leader of this chorus was the younger son, Franek, a handsome, well-trained tenor. And so we used to sing the old songs to our hearts' content in the midst of Siemens TV sets and Sony adapters.

Needless to say, I do not pride myself on my dubious nobility, for any moment I am apt to enroll, instantly and gladly, in the Wilno proletariat. Those categories were cheek by jowl over there. You had to have a good eye to tell a petty Polish noble from a Belorussian peasant. However, I should like to call to mind that entire social craft of narration, or better, the nobility's luxuriant culture of storytelling.

Well then, its peculiarity, that is, its aroma, charm, and lure, was free composition, and an interblending of subject matters and narrative wherewithal, perhaps even a certain pastiche quality, which reflected the way of thinking of those bisons and wild boars of the primal forest. That penchant for pastiche has stayed with me, too, and I delight in it when I write in a pseudo-Lithuanian style about my frailties and adversities.

Yet those informal tales, to which I claim kinship, stand out by the elegance of their language. For evidence one only has to look into the writings of Father Meysztowicz. So the language may well be the essence of the genre, which I, unworthy as I am, attempt to carry on after the departure of the legitimate "heirs and assigns" (as the old phrase went) into another world. And here, right here, the problem begins. I have always had trouble with the native language; here, too, some demon lies in wait for me. When a sentence that is juicy, dynamic, and pithy as a proverb issues from my pen, the professors instantly opine that it isn't good Polish. But when they apply their correction, that sentence withers, fades, and right away stops meaning anything. When some expression is correct it is clearly good for nothing; it only needs to be faulty to stay in your ear forever.

I mentioned Father Meysztowicz. He writes that the word *żagary*, which furnished the name of a prewar group of Wilno poets, signifies splinters, matchwood to use for kindling. In my family, now, and in my neighborhood, *żagary* was the term for the dry branches of shrubs. In my usage, *żagary* are something scratchy, thorny, that catches at your clothes. To burst through a stand of *żagary* was a difficult feat. Another thing that was called *żagary* was the dry, slender twigs of trees. Besides, *żagary* also served as kindling, for they made a dry tinder good for starting a fire with.

The worst of it, though, is that I don't remember what was meant by this word among the poets who used it as the watchword of their artistic manifesto.

Impatience

My misfortune is impatience. We are told that everybody has implanted in him the affliction destined to cause his death. Thus it is my belief that when the time comes I shall perish through my own impatience.

My impatience, though I am at great pains to conceal it, really is unbearable. If I decide on something, I have to carry it out at once. If I run into some problem, I have to solve it instantly, headlong. If I have an appointment I go crazy trying to wait out the time.

Impatience is an ague or trembling fit, inability to concentrate, perennial sleeplessness. At the moment, I am left to myself, my wife having gone abroad, so I have certain household duties to perform. The result of this is that I try to do all these things at once, because I am impatient. Boiling water for tea, getting dinner for Ivan, tearing off a calendar page, turning on the radio, taking medicine, washing a fork, and contemplating my hapless fate may at some juncture bring about total domestic mayhem.

It was this failing that compelled me to give up driving some time ago. I had to be the first to streak off at sixty from under the traffic lights, I had to overtake everybody, and with every trifling defect I would rush to the garage and implore them to attend to it immediately.

For my impatience is oddly linked with another failing—perfectionism. I simply cannot go to sleep knowing that there is oil leaking from the sump pan of my car; I fret all day if a button comes off my coat; I am ready to kill myself if I find a misprint in a book of mine, where they have put "neuralgia" instead of "nostalgia."

And what if a faucet starts dripping? What if a pen starts writing paler or darker? What if I get a summons from a government office? People had better move out of the house where I live then.

There is still another affliction deriving from impatience, and that is recklessness. I have been guilty of recklessness for years, I am simply dreadfully reckless.

To be imprudent in youth is nothing terrible. But in advanced years this vice is a menace. I don't need to adduce specific evidence here. My whole life has been frivolous. My whole literary output, if one may call it literary, has been astoundingly frivolous.

And now all of a sudden my hair stands on end as I recall a narrative I wrote a short while ago, which I am keeping under a bushel because something tells me that this product may deserve drowning in the nearest river. But of course I can't make myself do it: I am impatient and reckless. I'll pull it out from under the bushel and launch it into the world. I know this will come to a bad end for me. My Lithuanian canniness and painful past experiences tell me not to go public with this stillbirth; not to make a fool of myself in my old age; not to administer my own *coup de grâce*.

Tomorrow or the day after, though, I will of course spread out this repulsive flab of my gut, torn out of myself for no good reason, in front of hostile, grudging, or at best indifferent people.

I am reckless and impatient, you see. Impatient and reckless.

13

I don't believe that the number thirteen is unlucky, but I dislike it thoroughly. As a comprehensively educated and up-to-date person I disbelieve in superstitions from time to time. Right now I am going through a period, of unknown duration, of disbelief in anything one cannot scrutinize by reason.

The thirteenth day of the month is just the same sort of day as every other in the whole year. The thirteenth is simply a normal day, marked by the same number of accidents as the remaining days of the week, the same number of lottery wins, children being born, and old men dying. I can't help smiling at those weird, old-womanish, dumb prejudices against the thirteenth.

I smile—but very cautiously and furtively. Wouldn't it typically happen to an enlightened person like me that all misfortunes (modest ones at that) occurred to him on a thirteenth— and not at all on a Friday, actually.

For example, on a certain thirteenth, a Sunday, the dear doctor had a casual look into my Wilno throat and a few days later cut out a piece of my larynx along with some cancer.

Another time, I was cooking up a terrific deal. Jerzy Kawalerowicz and I had found a solid producer for the scenario we had written, based on Stanisław Dygat's *Travels*. There had been many months of fuss and commotion about this film project. Any number of producers and pseudo-producers had sniffed at the subject, thought about it, vacillated, and nothing had come of it all. We had sharpened the text of the scenario, not to say the shooting script, up one side and down the other, perfecting the plan of a future masterpiece.

And finally a taker turned up: a real go-getter in the film game, with cash, connections, and zeal to get started. We ran into him in Belgrade, where we had taken rooms in a splendid hotel, partook of gourmet lunches, and went on relaxing strolls, while our benefactor rooted among telex machines, held conferences with local studios, in a word, put out a lot of energy to rev up production. The season was spring, Easter time, Jerzy and I were on the loose, the deal practically signed and sealed, the contract money virtually rattling in our pockets.

Toward the end of our stay in this pleasant place, when everything pointed to a happy end, the producer stepped into our room one afternoon and laid the agreement on the table for us to sign. And we, lazy, without a care in the world, come back at him that we'll sign later and return the thing tomorrow.

He disappeared; we turned the pages of the contract over in our hands, stifling yawns, and laid it aside unsigned. There was time, tomorrow we would manage to calligraph our names on those sheets redolent of currency.

But before nightfall I took a look at the calendar, touched by some presentiment.

"You know what, Jerzy? Tomorrow is the thirteenth."

"You don't say," my partner responded without interest.

"It would be a joke if the deal blew up. Maybe we'd better sign before the day is out."

"Oh, come on. Superstition," Jerzy replied, and turned to the wall.

Next day, still in dishabille, we are consuming an elegant breakfast. There is a knock at the door, and our producer enters. Solemn, stiff, with a black file in his hand.

"*Leider,*" he says. "So sorry."

This accursed word is the worst expression in today's German language. The Germans often feed us this expression, and they are going to feed it to us more and more frequently.

So this ruddy, black-clad gentleman says "*Leider,*" and we feel we're dreaming, that this is simply the sort of mindless hallucination that comes as sleep dissolves. We pinch ourselves in every possible spot to wake up from this idiotic dream.

But it wasn't a dream. Dryly and dispassionately our all-but-benefactor informed us that some negotiations with prospective co-producers had come to nothing and that he had "*Leider*" to withdraw from the project; wherefore he was extending tender goodbyes to us and flying off to the fatherland, wishing us success in our future lives. His assistant would drive us to the airport and put us on a plane home. GOODbye.

This happened on a thirteenth in April. Of course I don't believe in those jinxed dates, but before the thirteenth I never tear off the calendar leaf. Everybody around is running into trouble with that thirteen, but in my house it's the twelfth. Yet however I put off that number, endeavor not to notice it or cannily forget it, still various petty, vexatious misadventures always befall me and sting like nobody's business. They have long seen through my ruses, they know my calendar trick by heart, and so they, too, make more and more use of the calendar: that· is, knowing I am not going to tear off tomorrow's leaf, they go to work the day before smashing glasses in my hands, scattering money from my pocket somewhere along the road, mailing letters I changed my mind about, setting friends against me.

Now I have again blundered into misfortune's jaws. In that book, the one I mentioned I had under my hat, I permitted myself so gross a provocation of the powers of bad luck that I don't expect to sleep quietly anymore, ever. What I have done is divide that hapless book—titled, I don't know why, *Under-*

ground River, Underground Birds—into thirteen chapters. I could have organized it into ten, fifteen, twenty sections, but I shaped it deliberately, with full premeditation, with complete awareness of the possible consequences, into thirteen chapters. I dressed that helpless victim of a book up in the shroud of thirteen. Over the wretched text I erected, like the cross over a grave, the symbol of that fiendish, hell-born thirteen.

That is why I can't sleep. That is why every night I hear that novel groan in agony in its drawer. That is why I shake like jelly, knowing that it will gather the remnants of its strength to crawl out of the drawer and, with my timid backing, fare forth into the world, that little New World of mine, and make me a laughingstock to the end of my days. But that mockery will not be tragic, will not take some pathetic shape, will not convulse the conscience of neighbors and passersby. It will be the quiet sort of flop. A bit of shrugging, a certain amount of compassionate head wagging, some whispers to the effect that he is finished, poor fellow.

Who thought up that thirteen!

My Pastimes in Film

Not wishing—or perhaps wishing—to brag, I may say that I was one of the first, for all I know the first, in Europe to launch that strange entity in movies that was dubbed *"auteur* film" or the New Wave in cinematography. These two terms were sometimes joined with reference to certain directors, but kept apart with others. By this time we know, however, that in the late fifties a veritable revolution—in filmic art, technology, and production—took place in European cinematography, completely transforming the face of the contemporary motion picture. I got in on this at the ground floor. I wrote *The Last Day of Summer* in '56 and filmed it with the Laskowski clan in '57. After that I drowned in the wave of imitators and eventually was very often called an imitator of my imitators.

Come to think of it, I had an amusing encounter with our fellowship of film critics. You see, in the early days it had tremendous creative ambitions. It was scientific, it was progressive, it was pregnant with culture, it was universal, global, and also infallible. I may now mention it without the reverence formerly due it, for it is gone. It has lost its teeth, sunk into dotage, and for the most part, following the normal course of events, died off.

Well, that ambitious and competent critical fraternity of ours simply overlooked me. They decided in their considerable conceit that my debut was one of those insignificant and inconsequential incidents: just a fault in the weft caused by an impudent outsider. Suffice it to mention that one of the newspaper reviews of *The Last Day of Summer* bore the title "A Chick and a Hunk on a Beach."

The insulted reviewing profession never forgave me subsequently; and what they held against me was the mere fact that they had overlooked me, had underestimated me, had failed to see what was going on. By the time my successors came around they were petted, practically rubbed sore with caresses in order to spite me, expertly coddled and cosseted, exalted to the cinematic sky. Whereas I was always smothered in silence. I was scarcely written up, and the tone was sour. Puffed up, they were, implacably resentful and cantankerous. They resented me for their own lack of discernment and laid the whip on me for their inability to identify in time the *nouvelle vague* they would later glorify. I was disqualified for jumping the gun.

But why do I write this? Some people will furrow up and proclaim severely that the author suffers from complexes, constantly complaining and griping. I deliberately wrote "furrow up" instead of "raise their eyebrows," using a homespun turn of speech that belongs to provincial squiredom and is apt to irritate Warsaw drawing-room society. But why am I writing all this? A rhetorical question. I have often posed rhetorical questions and received answers I didn't want. Many times I have expressed doubts I didn't harbor, often pretended ignorance of something in order to stir up the reader. Readers like to catch the author in inaccuracies, eagerly tick off mistakes for him, and I make this easier for them out of courtesy. I treat readers politely. I fawn on them.

I write about those beginnings of mine in film as of funny incidents, a fortuitous concatenation of circumstances which guided my film career this way and no other. All this was long ago, and perhaps I merely fool myself that things were then as I now imagine they were.

However, I had something else in mind. I meant to recall our pastimes in film those decades ago. For to me, practically a professional writer, film at that time was a sort of adventure, amusement, change of routine. To gain access to that tight little world was really no mean feat for a literary person. Here was a person from a rather reclusive specialty making his entrance among people of different professions, different levels of education, and different characters; he entered among them and became their boss, their dictator, their despot. This was a factory, a production plant, a military unit, and I became its director or general for six months.

You must remember that we were all young at the time. There weren't any old filmmakers, everybody was really having his debut. Young people, to their shame, like to take a drink and have fun. Accordingly, we, too, took drinks and had fun.

I remember how before one of my first films we took off to shoot locations and traveled several days through northern Poland. I found myself in the somewhat artificial situation of a writer going into directing. In other words, I was a tyro, and the "seniors" looked upon me with derision, whispered behind my back, and hinted broadly about a swig from the bottle. These solicitations, though, were not the result of intense thirst but, rather, tests of my character. My retinue was curious about the reaction of a Warsaw pensucker—a calling which they thought belonged to a subspecies of the milksop.

So we drove on our way through fields and forests in our demobbed Studebaker, and my fellows kept making remarks, while I, like a skinflint, a square, someone who is out of it, kept my mouth shut, stubbornly pretending not to hear this mild raillery.

Later we drive off for outdoor shooting. After the first working day we return in the evening—and find the tables set with snacks and savories, among which stand quart bottles of premium vodka beaded with frost. The crew went into ecstasy and hurled themselves into the fray.

At dawn the next day I do a round of our quarters with my cane and grumble at seeing none of the men ready for work. Presently they crawl out from somewhere, eyes red as white rabbits', hands shaking, lips chapped. Off we go to the forest to work.

That evening there are again tables with snacks and vodka. But the enthusiasm is less this time. They did eat and drink, though. The next morning they were hung over, sadness in their eyes; only I was vigorous, buoyant, full of humor.

A week later somebody scratches at my door at night. My assistant sidles in and gabbles something about his duodenal ulcer acting up again, and that he must request to be exempted from banquets, since he can't tolerate them. I roughly refuse permission. How can that be? After work you have to have a drink. No giving up.

A few days after that, one of the production assistants diffidently worms his way in, an old pachyderm that nobody could get the better of. Now he fixes me with a tear-drenched gaze, handing me a doctor's certificate. He, too, can't carry on, his hair has even begun to fall out. But I am adamant. What are they talking about, they love having a drink, I keep hearing about that, and here all of a sudden I get stuff about doctors, about hair falling out. That's absolutely out. Another banquet tomorrow.

They began to bring in children who clutched my trouser legs and cried. Wives came and tried bribery. More and more often I heard communal prayer. Still I did not give in. Even now some grizzled old film hounds will abruptly blanch at the sight of me and make squealing for the horizon.

Another time it was up to me to throw the traditional party to celebrate the close of shooting of my current film. Kazio Kutz had just been awarded a prize at an important festival, so he, too, was ready for a party. What I did was, I invited his crew to join mine and had tables set out in the canteen and a fine vodka—in those days we still had the wherewithal—put on ice.

So the little banquet got under way. And it went pretty briskly, for we were dealing with two crews who, like it or not, competed with one another, like two armies in the realm of art. The air thickened and I could sense a storm gathering: for right next to me I could see my assistant dance with Teresa, a tall, lovely actress, very young, known for her imagination and her tart temper; dance with her in a decidedly languorous pose, perhaps already on the sozzled side. And she, that minx of a Teresa (she got lost somewhere, I have lost track of her, and by now she would barely be a mature woman), she was holding over my assistant's balding head a sardine can full of leftovers of some sort, and slowly, carefully, fertilizing my man's pate. And it must be added that she was wearing Kazio Kutz's colors at the time, so that her gesture might be counted as one of disrespect for my crew.

Later I see her before me. She is sitting at the opposite side of the table and looking at me provocatively. She picks up a little platter of tomatoes and throws it to the floor, expecting an outburst of anger on my part. But I, without interrupting my conversation with my neighbor, pick up a dish of some wet mess and, whoosh, fling it over my shoulder. She goes for a decanter, I for a tureen. And so it went.

Until Wojtek Has's lot, who were there, too, grabbed the Soviet television set. That was where I drew the line. I wasn't going to give up the Soviet television set. The situation the day after had better be shrouded in silence. The infuriated abstainers photographed the premises, called the management, and raised hell, complaining that the workers in the art crew had overstepped the limits. But I outfoxed them; before anything could happen—like political restrictions—the place looked like new. Luckily, too, the director had been in high school with me. He had a little talk with me in his frigid office, I appealed to him on bended knees in approved old Polish fashion, and the affair passed into oblivion. For when all was said and done, the guzzling had been done by honest workers, after all, even though there had happened to be a few degenerates like myself among them.

We were young—when there was work we slaved our heads off, so from time to time we had to relax a bit. And at the time there wasn't any smack or snow or grass; we indulged in our native narcotic with the blue or red label.

I also remember a New Year's Eve which fell in the middle of a film job. More properly, I remember practically nothing about it except that I prepared it carefully, appointed it exquisitely, affectionately welcomed my crew, that is, my guests. And they began to raise their glasses to me, to drink to my health. I didn't want to fall into arrears, so I rushed to the forefront, although it wasn't eleven o'clock yet. As I rushed to the forefront I was suddenly shrouded in darkness. I woke up in the New Year, in considerable discomfort and amazed to be lying in my bed like a good child—or rather on my couch, while my festive garb hung in the wardrobe, elegantly draped; indicating that I had been carefully retrieved from under the banquet table and conveyed to my room with the solicitude due a person of a certain age.

Another little reception after another film lives in my memory, when at a certain point I saw in the passage a man cowering in an odd position, while a stream of horrifying white froth issued from his mouth, making him look like a great fire extinguisher in action, for the stuff kept oozing out of him forever, ready to go till morning, for all you knew.

the cat *Ivan pondering existence*

Eventually I was told that our electrician had imbibed a few too many and Kurt Weber, my well-beloved cameraman, had rendered him first aid. My shrewd Kurt had noticed that whenever I had taken aboard an excess cargo of firewater, the next morning I would take a quantity of big white pills. Observing his fellow worker in distress, and himself unschooled in matters alcoholic, he remembered my procedure. But he didn't remember, or perhaps had never noticed, that I dissolved these pills in water. So Kurt dragged his man to my room, found the bottle of pills, and with the best of intentions, seeking to hasten the delinquent's detoxication, shoved a whole handful of the pills down his throat. But this was Alka-Seltzer. People not averse to a drink know what that means. They need no explanation. To this day film people in Wrocław are haunted by the frothy vision of a human fire extinguisher.

You must know that those halcyon years of mine, my junkets in film, which adorned the tedious life of a literary man, coincided with the full bloom of the Warsaw Film Studios, a new, vigorous, spirited film outfit dominated by cheerful, energetic repatriates.

I shall always keep a warm place in my heart for that Wrocław, and for those studios, which were both workplace and lodging, for we all lived in the hotel wing there. Initially the hotel part was better than the studios, later the reverse was true. But it was always pleasant, congenial, and suffused with a great élan for work.

For a strange thing happened to this far-flung, green, damp city. The fact is that no other place, aside from Cracow and Warsaw, knew such an explosive burst of cultural activity as Wrocław after the war. How many extraordinary people issued from that city, though they were not natives of it; how many poets, writers, painters, musicians, filmmakers! Some mysterious constellation must have occurred there, perhaps two clouds, one European, the other Asiatic, or Eastern and Western, or Ruthenian and pristine Polish, some two such vast clouds must have collided above this city, releasing salvos of thunderclaps and blue streaks of talent.

It wasn't really my idea to recall those banquets, which are so frequent in Poland on various occasions, or in the least to irritate any devotees, believing or unbelieving. I simply meant to bring out that we were young in those days, there were simply a whole lot of young people who blew into flame the first little sparks of the art of Polish film—and no one knew what the future of this mirage, this gypsy illusion, would be, but our intentions were good, we wanted to join the current of world cinema, take the measure of the heroes of our childhood and early youth, Humphrey Bogart, Henry Fonda, or even Cecil B. De Mille—although all this was already a bit shopworn at the time.

How Artists Live

It seems to me that artists—by which I mean writers, composers, directors—observe each other stealthily, perhaps even askance, or possibly with a veiled little smile of sympathy; that although they may never meet, never exchange even a few words at a distance, never express an opinion of one another, there still is spun between them a thread of communality, an odd interdependence, a secret kinship. Given a long life—and people live rather long today, though lately they have again started to die oftener and younger—in the course of a long life one witnesses many of those artists' dramas: quiet, played out in silence, lived though with teeth clenched. The louder, more tragic ones you hear about from time to time, the ones that end in some scandal, some desperate rampage which might yet alter destiny, and those which end in death, suicide more often than not.

How many outstanding artists within my memory rose to the very acme of fame, and by now no one remembers them; I mean no one even knows of their existence, no one in the generations born a few years later! How many artists not in control of their talent reached their apogee too early, and for decades later glowed more and more faintly like an old prewar light bulb—there used to be a kind that wouldn't quite go out.

Or I see artists—I have in mind writers—who have worked up an original voice of their own, established their own writing technique, their own world or, better, poetic reality, and are unable to tear themselves out of their limited microcosm, cannot pull their heads out of the horse collar of their own making, find no escape from the trap they themselves have set.

I also see about me individuals who talk to themselves, imagining they are having discussions with their contemporaries. This is the awful phenomenon of an artist who has carried himself beyond term, who still blathers while his public has long left, has long passed into the other world; who does not realize that his galaxy has already completed half its elliptical round and what gazes at him now are other stars, other constellations.

Time rushes on head over heels, and so do we. Mann is dead, and no one reads Mann; Hemingway killed himself, and no one reaches for Hemingway; Sartre faded away, and no one knows any more who Sartre was.

It goes without saying that some dull pedant is now going to argue that his aunt does read Mann, and his old gramps is in raptures over Sartre. But I am talking about a certain tendency, certain phenomena not previously known; I am talking about the fact that the existence of traditional arts is in jeopardy. I don't assert that they will perish tomorrow or the day after, I merely say that they have come to feel threatened, and that sense of menace produces attacks of hysteria, raging fevers, and attempts at suicide.

To keep a foothold in the market today, to retain the favor of readers or spectators, demands an intense struggle. A master in this contest for a place on the cliffs of Parnassus was the late Buñuel. All his life he had a magical influence on the critics, he was connected with them by an invisible hot line; by some psychic aura unfathomable to outsiders he tyrannized these otherwise predatory Zoiluses. The worst piece of tedium he might happen to produce they would parade triumphantly around the world—a rather indifferent world, one might add.

Buñuel was not put off by this clamor about him, this unending claque. And all of a sudden, toward the end of his life, he began to make films for people, ordinary spectacles, even featuring little shticks for the less discriminating public. Needless to say, in all these pictures he burned some metaphysical joss sticks and had slender lines of fume wreathing across the screen to suggest to the audience some inscrutable mysteries and transpyrenean eschatologies. The public responded, but the critical reaction was so-so. So the maestro devised a curious dodge. He attended a major festival and let it be known that he had brought the last film of his life. In consideration of this, he was awarded the Grand Prix amid unusual ceremonies and, yielding to the entreaties of his worshippers, departed to make another film. In this way he produced three, perhaps five last films of his life.

I am not being sarcastic here, nor disrespectful to the memory of a great artist; all I mean to point out is that it is not sufficient today to produce high-quality art, one has to fight with tooth and claw to push it into the market and down people's throats. There are artists, to be sure, who bring this off.

We have had an explosion of blazing summer for a few days, followed by a return of bitchy cold and a sort of meteorological lethargy. The cat Ivan, who has grown fat on my rations and looks like a director, dogs my footsteps, demanding that I should serve as his warm mattress. He adores it when I withdraw into my niche (*neesh* is the current pronunciation, soon it may be *nitch* again, the linguists keep changing it) and lie down on my couch. He suddenly materializes from nowhere then, pretends to be just happening by, views the pictures on the wall, sniffs at the radiator, then abruptly with a high bound lands on my sorely tried belly. Next there is a bout of kneading, to the accompaniment of amiable purring; the cat looks for a good place to lie down on, describes one circle on my abdominal region, then another, at length thumps down heavily across my gut. Well, *à la bonne heure.*

My wife once saw the cat bite Ania, our daughter, fiercely on the wrist. The skin broke, blood squirted, but the child did not withdraw her hand from the little brute's jaws and calmly observed its savagery.

"Ania, why do you let him mangle your hand like that?" scolded my wife.

"Mama, Ivan needs to get something out of life, too," Ania answered indulgently.

Before Sleep

Today is the thirteenth. I didn't tear off the calendar leaf, of course, so in my house it is the twelfth. It is night, arctic temperature, rain pouring behind the panes and drumming on the sill, and I am awaiting the midnight, and so is the cat, that will make the fiendish thirteen pass—which I don't believe in, but which has been known to bring me bad luck now and then.

About midnight, sure enough, I begin to feel queasy. In the Wilno country, where we used to go to bed at eight, or before nine in cases of festive dinners and entertainments, midnight was a mysterious, awesome, actually terrifying time, and I don't remember making it till midnight—and being conscious of it— in childhood or early youth. As a child I thought that midnight was altogether unendurable, and I prayed many times that sleep might cover over this fearful threshold of time, that awful spell when the churchyards release the wicked and the hapless, and evil spirits, apparitions, and cadavers.

I hope that what I am going to say will not sound like profanity, but it is a fact, an arresting fact to me, that many times in my life, not only in childhood but in mature years and now on the verge of old age, I have dreamed of the Devil, of Satan; whereas God, whom after all I believe in and have never disavowed to the best of my knowledge, has never appeared to me in a dream; that is, I have never in my sleep sensed His presence, His light, His sanctity. Of course you may put the blame on me, find shortcomings and sins in me, ill will or inadequate goodwill, but after all, a person cannot be held responsible for his dreams, regardless of the fact that they supposedly influence his waking life. One surely cannot be made to answer for what happens to one in that unknown dimension or unexplored reality to which he undertakes voyages, or perhaps pilgrimages, daily between midnight and dawn.

So many times have I myself awakened with a scream, tortured by evil powers I could not see and couldn't have described but which I was aware of, which I felt with all my senses next to me in the murk, in darkness, in a horrifying shadow. And I have frequently heard of others who also knew that heavy awakening to a groan or a dreadful sigh, as if they were clawing their way out of an abyss.

But perhaps it is at one's last moment that one dreams of God. Perhaps there is no more return then to our sinful, miserable, cruel world of everyday.

Yes—somewhere high above us, above the rain and freezing wind, Midnight passes. She probably passes with a limp, chilled, blowing into her hands, wearied by this ceaseless migration; passes above this town, which has become my town, passes and travels westward until she reaches Danka, my wife, and Marysia, my daughter, who are having tea in the Warsaw manner and only then, on the island of Manhattan, become aware of the approaching night, which bears a fragment of memory from me, a human reflection of the divine power.

Something makes me run forward, headlong, with such terrible force. But what?

Holidays

I pace my apartment, prowl back and forth, I am beset by boredom, by loneliness, so I mosey hither and thither, look out the window, where I see a very familiar middle-sized apartment house with a tiled roof, and on the left a geometrically laid-out stand of poplars, which grow year by year like mad and have long hidden the view of the hideous cinder-gravel parking lot and will hide the sky before much longer. I walk, promenade, prowl about the apartment, inspect the familiar walls, the sickly greenery dangling from clay pots, the pictures hanging slightly askew—and suddenly I notice that on the shelf holding my own books, where maps, plans, photographs, and postcards are painstakingly located, solidly emplaced, deeply embedded, one picture postcard has left the ranks on its own, broken from concealment, and set itself up leaning against the books reverse side to me (for formerly people said "obverse or reverse" instead of "head or tail"), turned its back to me to make me notice it, having popped out like a pebble from the sand no one knew how or when; so I become aware of it, move up close, take the yellowed, grimy little card into my hands, and see that the right-side view is a panorama of Wilno before the First World War, and on the reverse someone has written in blue ballpoint-pen calligraphy: "1978. May Our Lady of Ostra Brama watch over us. Staś."

I hold this postcard in my hand, a terribly old postcard which Staś Dygat sent me for the New Year, the New Year of 1978 and a month before his death. I had forgotten about this postcard, may well have forgotten it already in 1977, a day or two after receiving it. And here it had worked its way out from among survey maps of the province and city plans of Warsaw, pushed out from the tight squeeze of photographs and old postcards people have sent me, breaking loose from its durance by an uphill struggle as if from a grave, from a country churchyard, and took me by the hand—or rather, Staszek did. Staszek, that bum, who suddenly left us, his colleagues, when things were hottest, when so much had happened and was still happening, that Staszek, who has been dead six years, has come to see me all of a sudden in the likeness of that apostrophe to Our Lady of Ostra Brama, on his birthday—for one of these days, or right about now, is his name day, which we used to observe in great style; but now he has gone off on the longest journey and we, his buddies, feel out of sorts somehow; Staszek seems to have played a trick on us, left us at some gate and vanished. We keep waiting and waiting, but it's no good; sometimes Kalina, his wife, passes by in her black cape, that's all. I look at that post-card, the side known as the right or obverse, and I see a faded image of a provincial Wilno, and towering over it a huge white cathedral I don't remember, which wasn't there anymore in the thirties, when I used to be in Wilno for unseemly amusements and later "frequented" (as it used to be called) the King Zygmunt August High School. How, then, did that Russian Orthodox edifice get into this antique photograph? Perhaps the Tsars at some point erected these monuments to their glory in cities of rebellious spirit.

Staszek has gone. He was struck from the roster of the living, of those who go to dinner, are in love, quarrel with their colleagues, and go on vacation. And we journeyed to Kazimierz, at the beginning and near the end of the fifties. This little town on the Vistula, crammed against the river by hills and buttes scored by ravines, a little burg built centuries ago by Italian artisans, who have left their vestige to this day in surnames of inhabitants like Doraczyński, from Dorazzi, or the broadly disseminated Pisulows, from Pisulo.

This Kazimierz was renowned before the war, when the painters discovered it. I shall always see before my eyes Nasfeter's film *A Woman Unloved*, and specifically its opening sequence, the views of Kazimierz with those figures of Jews frozen in midgesture. But these are not so-called stills, they are live takes, with birds flying in the sky, branches moving with the wind, a dog running across, and everywhere, in foreground, background, and middle distance, Jews standing congealed forever in the postures in which their ruin overtook them.

We in turn must have been drawn to Kazimierz after the war

by painters, perhaps my friend and ours, Miecio Piotrowski, graphic artist and writer, or perhaps someone else tempted us, lured us, persuaded us. That first trip of ours with Danka and little Marysia was actually a failure. I remember that I had a hard time securing through the editors of *New Culture*, where I was working, a wagon to convey my wife, the child, and their traps to the summer place, where I had booked a room in a boardinghouse rented out by the state travel bureau. Our engine wasn't broken in, so we were on the road all day, and later half the night, as, having left Danka and Marysia in Kazimierz, I returned with the little old driver, who wasn't broken in himself, or perhaps totally broken down.

Next morning I had hardly opened my eyes, hardly begun to make up my mind on how to organize a happy bachelor's life, when the telephone rings and it's Danka in despair. Marysia, a year-old tyke, hasn't stopped howling all night long. Everyone is going crazy, the neighbors, the staff, and the luckless mother.

So I rush to Kazimierz, by train, by bus, on foot, any way God will grant. I remember nothing of this first encounter; a wooden summer house, a partition of lightly planed boards, and screaming Marysia's gaping maw. But later there were splendid outings, excursions in the spring, in the summertime, even in winter. Marysia grew bigger; Ania was born, who did not howl but who fell down every few minutes, so Danka had to carry a small pharmacy along to treat scuffed knees. And I in the meantime got hold of an automobile; actually, it was my father-in-law, Alfred Lenica, who got it, but it was I who drove the old rattletrap, some sort of antediluvian Morris Oxford which scared me to death. I was in a panic, too, at those practically transoceanic voyages, those perilous expeditions through metropolises like Garwolin, Ryki, Żyrzyn, and Puławy. For Ania got sick every few moments, obliging me to stop my junk pile, hung all over as it was with electrostatic amulets and chains designed to neutralize local electric currents injurious to a child. Overdosed with antinausea tablets, stuffed with variegated mixtures recommended by compassionate friends, poor Ania proceeded with dreadful persistence every other mile or so to sacrifice to St. Vomitus.

Still, when we finally made it, there opened before us a new alluring world of the south, of Mediterranean culture and civilization, a magic island of crazy painters in the sea of drab everyday.

However, I must have written several times before about Kazimierz and sojourns shared there with Staszek and other friends, about blazing summers and sudden floods in the midst of summer, about movies set up in the church, and the pub called Berens for tradition's sake, about various nocturnal drinking bouts, volleyball of an evening, and the fact that I was always standing in the middle of the town square, near the well, planted there entire mornings, afternoons, and evenings, might as well call it whole days, waiting for who knows what. Actually, I constantly wait for something in my own house, too, but at home I wait more easily and gently, whereas on a trip, God forbid, on a trip I wait aggressively, with all my might, with a fierce passion.

I wrote about all this because I had already written on all that is worth writing about. What I haven't produced for a long time is the kind of writing everybody likes: Let's have a lot of action, make them love each other, make it all end happily. I understand the reader, I even sympathize with his tastes, but am not in a position to indulge him anymore. I have been demoralized, driven in another direction, where I don't have to take undue account of the predilections of my benefactors. If I had been pushed at the outset into a naturalistic mode of narration, the "slice of life" business in the true manner of the nineteenth-century novel, who knows but that I might now have palaces and motor yachts waiting the year round for my appearance at the port of the Grand Duchy of Monaco.

Augustów is another subject I have written about—the place where it was the fashion to vacation in the mid-fifties and early sixties. From the little station on the narrows between the lakes one made one's way by peasant cart, kids and baggage and all, to town, where we would stay at kind, dear Mrs. Alejster's for a month or two. I was there again three years ago and didn't recognize the little town: asphalt, concrete, and in the place of "the planks," the wooden open-air platform where we used to

dance on cool or sweltering evenings, they had even put up
something like a skyscraper. This modernization had contributed little to the hamlet's charm. It had lost its rustic character
and now resembled a municipal housing development or a Soviet resort on the Baltic.

But from the Augustów we knew, when the countryside was
still empty, we used to set forth on great forays into the woods
for berries and mushrooms. We paid visits to Przewięz, where
a tiny settlement between lakes, by an archaic sluice lock, held
an encampment of fledgling actors, who are now the luminaries
of our theater. It goes without saying that we played volleyball,
did some necking, and, in my case, shared some poaching—
illegally fishing of a misty morning on White Lake—with a certain champion of our theater, a great actor given to character
parts. I write about my partner in oracular language in order
not to cast aspersions on his name. Here I find myself writing
"cast aspersions," one of the drabbest locutions of the sort used
in every stupid paper by every half-baked journalist. Yet subtle
stylists like myself sometimes enjoy decorating their prose with
a bedraggled little phrase like that. I, as it happens, like to
overuse the pronoun "I," even to start a sentence with it in my
carefree way, although there is a slight whiff of Russicism about
it. I become shameless, since sham and fakery flaunt themselves
all about. If I commit some offense against grammar or syntax,
the professors raise cain and take me severely to task. But when
some cabinet minister belches something out in a horrible jargon that pollutes the spirit of Polish, it is said that we are dealing
with the trend of the contemporary language, with a process of
democratization, working-class language, and so on and so forth.

Another thing I think I have mentioned is that during this
Augustów time, or should I perhaps say this Augustan age, I
suffered from a perennial infection of the inner, or possibly the
middle, ear. Every fortnight, already totally deaf, I betook myself with those poor ears to a famous laryngologist, who with
the aid of a lovely wife made some cuts within these ears, causing
a terrific discharge, and of course prescribed big doses of pen-
icillin. This went on for several years. The only sweetener was
that doctor's beautiful lady, who each time put a nelson grip on

me with her lovely round arm to keep me from breaking loose during the procedure and running away.

So, one summer in Augustów, as I trudged dolefully among the sunbathers and swimmers with my cauliflower ears, plodded without hearing anything, not even a thunderclap during a storm, plodded too warmly dressed what's more, with a foolish smile on my face because I couldn't understand what was said to me: at a certain moment I was suddenly seized first by despair, then by a feral rage. Either I am going to do something about these ears, I told myself, or I'll stab myself, or simply drown myself in Lake Necko.

Well then—toward evening I made my way to the local hospital, where I was received by an impassive middle-aged physician. He had the same name as friends of mine in the Wilno Colony, so I asked him about it, but he wasn't related to them, nor had he ever laid eyes on the Colony.

After the procedure he told me, talking with a slight Wilno accent, that I should stop up my ears when bathing, with cotton if nothing else. He said this without conviction somehow, making it sound like a quack's recipe or some withered herbalist's advice. But I, glued to the wall by those hapless ears (a pretty image, that), heeded his advice and over the next thirty years never suffered from earache, knock-knock-knock on unpainted wood.

In the mid-sixties began the era of Chałupy, "The Huts," a humble little village about the middle of the Hel Peninsula in the bay of Gdańsk. By now this has turned into a huge resort area, the mecca of nudists from East Germany and all over Poland, a great practice range for deviants, perverts, and sexual eccentrics.

But when I happened there, it was still a quiet and modest place. Bathing in the sea, long walks with the actor Andrzej Łapicki, leisurely chats; and at five in the afternoon, right on the chime of Big Ben, Andrzej would appear on the balcony of his room and declaim in his characteristic voice: "Happy hour!"

I eagerly clambered up to his hermitage, and he with a kindly smile plunged his hand into a bucket of water and pulled out a carefully cooled half pint of pure vodka—for in those days people still drank neat vodka and nobody ever died of it. The sea rumbled at night, and to its rumble I slept like a dormouse. In the morning, or rather after lunch, I made my way to the scanty ribbon of forest, which was twenty or thirty yards wide here, and by the power of illusion imagined that I was walking by an ancient forest trail through the Kashubian wilderness, that any moment I would meet a Pomeranian demon. Beyond the dunes raged the stormy sea, but here it was tranquil, unknown birds winged by between the pine trunks, at times a startled hare leaped among the tall forest flowers. And I studied this forest, which had probably been planted with scientific patience by some German gamekeeper. Everything grew here, transported from all of Europe—alpine plants and swamp plants and desert plants and garden ones. All this botanical hodgepodge lived in harmony on a ribbon of sandy soil as slim as a baguette. This Lilliput forest was my very own enclave, my magic garden, and my Lithuanian wilderness.

But eventually Chałupy, too, went to the dogs. First one had to give up the walks along the beach to Kuźnica. So many years Andrzej and I had marched down the damp hard-beaten sand, rinsed by tenuous sun-warmed ripples, had wandered daily between ten and twelve, and everyone knew about this; fishermen, border guards, sea mews, the summer people, too, knew our habit of many years' standing. Until one year nudists arrived, and not some species of artistic wild men at that, but solid German burghers, followed by the Polish working class. And it turned out that even in these circumstances Andrzej caused a sensation. And so when time and again naked steelworker lasses or mining girls stepped into our path, possibly a little too close to the skin, Andrzej gritted his teeth and silently lengthened his steps. And next day he stopped our walks. This is how the chief attraction Chałupy held for us perished. For I, too, gave up those outings in the spumes of tiny droplets from the diffusing surf, which now and then burst into lovely succulent rainbows. In this way my range of possessions shrank once again.

For we stopped going to Chałupy. Those turbulent nocturnal revels ended; so did cooling one's heels at the grocery kiosk;

so did the nightly bombing runs by military planes practicing on some shanties on the estuary; so did being ripped off by greedy fishermen. One more thing passed slowly into oblivion.

And now I don't feel a need for vacations. Actually, I never did need them, because I am never tired. The simple fact is that nothing wears me out as much as doing nothing. Perhaps I never managed to learn to vacation, because the custom did not take root in me in childhood and youth. And the reason it did not was that I was constantly on vacation, for eighteen years I had a perennial summer resort on the Wilenka, in the loveliest river gorge in the world, the most marvelous nest lined with dark-green velvet, where streams of various mineral springs had their origin, where there rose from the primeval herbs unheard of, or better yet, unbreathed, the best air in the world, which even President Mościcki, Poland's President before the war, who invented canned air, might have a coughing fit over. We didn't have to go to summer resorts: the wretched rich from all over Poland came faring to us.

I don't know why, but Janek Brzechwa comes to mind, who of late has been living through a splendid second life, a true afterlife, and all of us, his friends and near ones, and acolytes as well, rejoice in his posthumous glory. Janek, then, when already advanced in years, used to say: The only pleasure I have left now is work.

Snows Sky-high

A hirsute young man turned up with long, curly hair and glasses screening bright eyes, which peered inquiringly but made no contact with an interlocutor's gaze. A little more than medium height, lean, skin and bones, as we used to say—veins, tendons, and bones, actually. He was dressed in a colorless sweater, and in this sweater and a skimpy linen or denim jacket he braved summer blazes as well as early frost. This fashion of presenting himself did not have to do with poverty; it was chic, style, perhaps a demonstration, certainly a kind of uniform, the colors, in the old sense of the word, which testified to your belonging to some sort of mafia, perhaps artistic, perhaps athletic, perhaps ideological. He came to me in the early spring of 1971 and stayed seven or eight months.

This was Stanisław Latałło, a young cameraman I had had my eye on because he was the son-in-law of friends and the son of a charming woman, a painter I had been to school with. After fourteen years much has grown hazy in my recollection; in general, for a literary man I have a weak memory. Perhaps it wasn't I who picked him out, perhaps he was brought to me by Jahoda, the cameraman of *So Far and Yet So Near*, who was his teacher in film school. Whichever way it was, he joined my crew and we began to work together.

He didn't talk at all, only answered questions, in monosyllables. He was probably on my assistant's budget, but had got a second camera from Jahoda with which he shot the digressions, commentaries, and glosses so frequent in this film, which was meant as an essay, a set of digressions, commentaries, glosses. Kodak film being in short supply, he filmed those bits on the ORWO film tape made in the German Democratic Republic. One day he showed me something he had done as a training exercise, a very sophisticated, multidimensional little piece he had done on that same ORWO film. Jahoda told me at the time that Staszek had long searched for this outdated and yellowed tape in the storehouses; precisely this "sick" or "soured" tape was appropriate for his experiments. I was enraptured by this little original. I had to have it. I wanted to have it forever, like a picture. So I spliced it into the film—it was *So Far and Yet So Near* we were doing at the time, I recall. And there it is, lodged in this film forever, or until the negatives fall apart. It is welded to the place at the very end of the film where the scene of the Calvary procession fades out.

One day Jahoda, who had clearly taken a liking to Staszek, tells me that his pupil had made an invention in the field of solarization. And since we were trying to find a way to shoot the scene of the Jew flying over the town, that special effect, this Polish solarization patent, struck us as superbly apropos. So that fragment of Staszek's was soldered onto our film.

And what he brought us from town and from the Polish countryside, what he cranked up with his second camera, always enraptured us. It depicted the same reality, as it were, that constituted the basis of the film; yet at the same time that reality appeared somehow enhanced, marked with a seal of magic, as though seen through the eyes of an otherworldly being.

I am not exaggerating in the least. This stringy, bearded boy harbored some mystery, and I am unable to decipher it, cannot give it a name, although I constantly see him before me, see him in motion, soundlessly running, for he was always moving and I was always chasing him, because I kept needing him; I needed not merely his attendance but also his opinion, his aesthetics, his eye. Also his approval—although I was somewhat embarrassed by this dependence on him.

In my film *So Far and Yet So Near*, which is after all a film of Mieczysław Jahoda's, too, there reposes a whole heritage of Stanisław Latałło, the young filmmaker who will never shoot another film. I do know of his other pieces, of things begun and not completed, which certainly are important testimony to his gift; but from this film of ours, owing to a peculiar context, perhaps through my foreboding and tenderness toward him,

through some strange correlation of two neighboring generations, his artistic achievement, the thrilling gleam that augurs
an extraordinary personality, will always radiate with a peculiar
power of humanity amid the brushwood of my own distractions,
complexes, and failures. I have encountered several such people
in my life before who were like beings from another planet.
They amazed you, intrigued you, shone in your eyes with a
supernatural luster, and departed this world like ordinary
mortals.

Staszek, too, departed as an ordinary person, although the
manner of his leaving was uncommon. I am saying that he left
as an ordinary person, for surely Staszek Latałło over there in
the Himalayas, where he was cameraman to an arduous expedition of Polish explorers, meant to conduct himself like a genuine human being; that is, with loyalty toward his fellows and
honesty toward his work. It was probably a certain inner max-
imalism, moral and artistic, that made him behave as he did.
And pay for it with his life; with his death.

I was asked after his death to write an occasional memoir
about him. I didn't do it. Yet I knew I would write it one day,
I would write it when the need arose. Whenever I see the
sparkle of a star in the sky, the lights of an airplane coursing at
the rim of the stratosphere, or the glow of sunrise or sunset, I
always remember that in those tallest mountains of our little
globe, amid those summits touching an unfathomed sky, among
those eternal snows there rests forever, after a short, unfulfilled,
tragic life, Staszek Latałło, a young Polish filmmaker, who like
no one else comprehended the tragic quality of our existence,
lost among the fire and ice of the cosmos.

The Word

I turn on the radio: a piano recital. I switch to the second
program: a piano recital. I change to the third: a piano recital.
I press the fourth button: a piano recital. Another time I ner-
vously run through all the channels, or rather gutters, of our

radio—and get the same news. Some other time all Warsaw stations offer a political chat. And almost always and at any time, all the channels have some phony affairs to attend to, some simulated concerns, some fabricated movement and fictitious energy.

A newcomer, traveler, foreign tourist would think that these programs are designed and composed by idiots, the protagonists of "Polish jokes." Yet we know, after all, that the author of radio and television programs, and also the editor of many newspapers, is the Cult of the Word. Some insane belief in the word, which came to us who knows from where, torments us twenty-four hours at a time, sows devastation in the country, drives us into crises and sudden revolts. For after all, in all those upheavals which we witness every fifteen years or so, an immense reportorial share of guilt is borne by that accursed twaddle, that blabber, that relentless blizzard of words.

I remember saying something critical about the nightly news broadcast to one of the chiefs of television, to Janusz Wilhelmi, to be precise. He pushed his glasses up on his forehead, looked at me half quizzically, half pityingly, and said: "You watch the TV news? I don't."

So they hold forth for hours at a time on TV and radio to viewers and listeners, but themselves couldn't care less. Yet surely they know perfectly well, living among people as they do, after all, that these people don't watch or listen either. The radio is on for hours, the TV dins all day, torrents of words, information, admonition, exhortation, oration, indoctrination, deviation, aberration, a Niagara of spavined Polish words, misstressed, wretchedly mispronounced, pour into a void, for during that time everybody is taking a bath, eating, sitting on the can, picking his nose, or copulating if young enough.

I remember July 1980. Great factories already stand idle, half of Poland is on strike, the whole society is in ferment, while every evening on the news there blooms on the screen the collected, competent, omniscient countenance of the presiding officer instructing, warning, educating, and summoning us to rhythmic, effective labor. If that doesn't show a touching faith in the power of the word . . .

And later, when all of Poland is seething, TV discloses the

First Secretary's face. He, too, with unction and in full consciousness of the weight of his appearance, summons us all to rhythmic, effective labor. If that doesn't argue confidence in the power of the word . . .

That same invaluable Wilhelmi proved possessed of a superb sense of the socialist dialectic during a session of some script commission. The discussion dealt with a text in which the authors on some occasion of dramaturgical weight showed prisoners working on streetcar tracks. Here Wilhelmi pipes up that this is a mistake, because in cities prisoners are not employed at such labors.

The director of the future film, who sat by the window, called the dignitary's attention to the fact that right then alongside the television buildings a gang of prisoners was working on the tracks.

Wilhelmi went to the window, pushed his glasses up on his forehead, observed the prisoners, and said: "It's not true."

I am listening to the radio in the morning. The announcer says that the sun is shining, it's warm and a good time for a walk. I see, though, that it's raining cats and dogs and a penetrating chill is spreading. But what is outside the window is unimportant. What is important is the word. The word is the ruler, the tyrant. The word is the reality despite reality.

Each new outfit that seizes the helm of state announces a brake on speeches, oratory, statements. But don't bet on it—six months later their tongues wag, they jabber, they wear you out by the hour. There was to be a sportscast, but we get a government statement. The program guide bills a detective story, the screen brings a lecture. There was to be a variety show; what we get is a speech. Yet everybody knows, after all, that this twaddle only makes things worse, that it enrages people, raises their hackles against the most sensible propositions, that it practically drives them into the street.

For whose benefit do we organize these daily talkathons? For whom do we every day smother the country with millions of tons of deflated, totally valueless words? For whose sake did we play the fool with all these words, make laughingstocks of them, strip them of their meanings, their power, their beauty?

I know that Mr. Censor has been squirming on his stool for a good while now. Every moment he reaches for his blue pencil to put an exclamation mark here, underline a whole sentence there, mark a spot of pollution at the margin elsewhere. I know that Mr. Censor is now wrestling with competing thoughts: to take out the whole section or only delete what might offend or incense somebody or even provoke a telephone call.

But I am fair-minded. I only write what has to be written. I myself know best how I should be censored. I spent half my life censoring myself, and in the present book, too, I undertook self-censorship. This self-censorship, like dope in horse racing, is to increase a hundredfold my puny creative powers. All those throttles, bolts, bungs, hoops are to impart new vim to my rarefied inner potency. Self-command, censorship by my own hand, should step on the gas to speed onward that one and only tome which will complete the trail of my confessions, my self-unmasking trilogy, my gravestone, which falls into three parts and crumbles into gravel.

I call upon everyone to embrace the sacred virtue of silence. Shut the words up in a dark place and let them rest. Let there be founded a multileveled state award for non-speech, non-statement, non-summing-up. By way of a good example I myself vow to lay my words to rest and not drag them across the pages of my impious books for three years. During these three years I will go on long walks, work "rhythmically and effectively," smile, dream, scratch my head. And only toward the end of 1987 shall I come forth with a word that will be new, unsoiled, expressive, beautiful, almost holy. I shall come forth with it if I live long enough.

Old Age

Old age is the negative of childhood. It takes a lot of trouble to crawl onto the scene of this life and a dreadful effort to crawl off.

I notice that a hole has developed in my teeth. I ought to see the dentist. But is it worth it? It won't be long now . . . I see in a store a beautiful raincoat. Should I buy it? There's no point. It won't be long now . . . I get horribly kicked around here, there, and everywhere. They leap for my head and throat in the literary stock market. The thing to do would be to hang myself under Poniatowski Bridge. But would it be worth the trouble? It won't be long now . . .

I swear, this old-age business is a rotten idea. Let's assume there has to be a terminus to our existence, which I am not at all ready to concede; let's say nature hadn't thought up a better alternative, then the end could at least be more aesthetically pleasing, less tormenting and prolonged. Add to this that for some lucky stiffs this annihilation proceeds lightning-swift and without suffering, while to other luckless ones fate (I am afraid to say accident), cruel fate allots a hideous, inhuman agony spread over months and years.

I used to think I would weasel out of old age. I lived in such stormy times. A sudden, unexpected death was so easily come by. Many colleagues, friends, rivals (but rivals for what?) had already departed smoothly into the star-sparkling blackness above us, and I was left like a tardy traveler on a deserted platform.

And then, Mother of God, there is that awful Lifeline on my right palm; it completely cuts across the bottom of the palm, climbs on top, creeps to the wrist, the elbow, the armpit. I can't stand this anymore. I am barely breathing. I suffer from some sort of intellectual hiccups, or psychological burps, I don't know. I am already short of the oxygen of patience, humility, concil-iation, and here a whole life is still before me. With such a Lifeline as I have, like a full spool of thread, I may live twenty, thirty, even fifty more years. Lord, have mercy upon me.

I was told by Irena Szymańska, a confederate at my table in the Czytelnik café, which table and its regulars are such a thorn in the side of government and opposition spheres, I was told by her that on the gravestone of Waclaw Nałkowski at the Powązki cemetery an inscription is carved which is a quotation from his works: "Nature, nature, I am grateful to thee for life."

There spoke the nineteenth century. We, from the end of the twentieth, look upon this nature, our own and that of an ever more distinct cosmos, with eyes bulging from horror and pain.

A Day at Janusz's

Sometimes, for no particular reason, Janusz Grabiański comes to my mind, a prominent graphic artist who died suddenly at an early age, in the flower of his years or at the height of his powers, as they used to say, at the acme of his success, his life tidy and harmonious in peaceful surroundings, among people who loved him and animals attached to him.

In the matter of people loving him I probably exaggerated a little, for at one time some of my wife's fellow graphic artists denounced her for a modest preface to a catalogue of a Grabiański exhibition which I, hapless creature, had composed at the time in a temperate vein.

Most people liked him; another sort, though, twisted creatures starved for approval and affection, envied him cordially and doggedly. But another's jealousy, surely, cannot alter a fate and thrust a person into the precipice.

I have strayed off course—I hadn't any intention of writing of people unworthy of the merest mention. I meant to say a few words about my sensitive, affectionate friend Janusz and his companions, who prowled the yard and orchard surrounding his hermitage, that comfortable workplace in the middle of his lot, a few steps from the house in the Warsaw suburb of Józefow.

So one time we were having fun with Kubuś, a parakeet, I forget his ornithological niche, which Janusz had taken over from his mother for safekeeping, or perhaps for a vacation in pleasant surroundings. Kubuś was fun, he had a sense of humor and an IQ worthy of a cabinet secretary. Janusz put on some jazz record and Kubuś, terrifically musical as he was, started shifting sideways along the perch in his cage as if cranking

himself up, and then took to whistling so beautifully and with
such a quality of musical invention that he sounded as if he
were Louis Armstrong in person. You could tell that Kubuś
adored those solos with a good rhythmic section and that he
cared particularly for American bands. Kubuś would entertain
us for quite a while with his concerts for flute, penny whistle,
or reed pipe; then Janusz would call him out of the cage. The
parakeet was reluctant to venture into freedom, clearly not used
to the new place yet. We sat down at the table and Kubuś came
with us; he didn't sit down, though, but flew around us, chat-
tering to himself, imitating Janusz's mother's voice and repeating: Kubuś, Kubuś, my sweet little birdie. Sometimes he would
alight on Janusz's shoulder and pick a tasty morsel from his lips.

After lunch we were going to go out into the garden and take
Kubuś along, so Janusz started to shoo him back into the cage.
But he hit upon a stubborn vein in the little bird. Kubuś started
teasing his foster father, pestering him, playing rascally tricks
on him. He would zoom by just over his head, dive under his
arm, flit between his fingers, and take evident delight in his
prowess.

In the end he obeyed, though. He went back into the cage
like a good bird, skipped onto his perch, and was carried into
the garden. There we lay down on the sun-warmed grass, a
meadow dotted with milkweed, for it was spring. We set the
cage with Kubuś down between us and began a lazy postprandial
chat. Kubuś took part in our conversation, using his human
voice, tilting his little head, sidestepping on his wooden rod.

At that point, though, a new interlocutor turned up. He was
an alley cat by the name of Wujek, a regular bandit all covered
in scratches, scars, and bald spots left from fur ripped off by
rivals. This Wujek, then, local hooligan well known all over the
neighborhood but also a tom with a golden heart, started to
take an intense interest in the conversation. He became so
involved that he jumped onto the cage in order to hear and see
better. He settled in an uncomfortable position on the steel
wires of the cage roof and fixed his gaze on us with a devotion
suggesting that he would be disconsolate to miss even a single
word of our discourse. He veritably ingested the substance of

our reasoning with his whole being, yearning only for instruction, his only hunger the hunger for knowledge.

Yet suddenly I become aware that this reprobate, while simulating absorption and affecting to impart to his scarred little mug a mien of sophisticated intellectualism, is insinuating his right paw between the rods of the cage, lowers it more and more, unsheathes his claws, and clearly intends to seize Kubuś, who like a well-bred gentleman politely keeps his distance from these strange advances. What I want to stress is that Wujek looks at us steadily throughout all this, not taking his eyes off us for a second, operating his paw blindly, yet very effectively.

There isn't going to be any payoff to this. The cat got a cuff on his bony hindquarters and fled home to a belated lunch. I am telling about this spring day and Janusz's two friends for my own pleasure, in order to recall that pleasant time and its mellow feelings, to smother the all-blackening ache that foisted itself upon life one fateful moment, the damnable ache it may take three lives to live down.

The less I like people, the more I like animals. Every aging curmudgeon is apt to say so. But this must have been what Hitler, too, told himself in his mind. For every tyrant loves animals but hates people. (Although Joseph Vissarionovich had no crush on animals, either.)

Apostrophe to the Censor

I repose such confidence in the censorship. Voluntarily do I slip into its yoke, for I look forward to some extraordinary effects from my asthmatic writing. At one time I did not fare badly under the censor's tender hand, some little successes were even scored . . . Censor, dear censor, help a poor, aging scribe!

But even the censor can't pour from an empty barrel . . .

Sunday

Right from dawn, the day was in a state of travail: now springlike, now wintry, then autumnal, finally bursting out in summer. I lay supine in an unwonted, alarming torpor, the deafness of Sunday morning, and looked at the window, which showed, as always, that northwestern sector of the sky, a quarter bowl of the oxygen tent in which we have been living so long and so lately. In the crack of the window, the chink through which I spy the sky, the stars have faded and shy little clouds like swarms of white doves have been appearing and floating by; later the poplars began to bend earthward, the air darkened rapidly, mountains of blue-black cloud billowed up, rain, or rather hail, drummed briefly on the sill, the weather darkened and lightened, someone turned the radio on and off again; I lay there and once more chewed on those barren thoughts which always float up at dawn or early morning and sought to overcome in my mind those sudden, strange, indescribable panics, anxieties, terrors—certain emotional states, moods, presentiments from the borderland between familiar reality and the mystic cosmos, which takes on sharper outline and emerges more and more clearly like a photographic print in the developing tray, to loom heavily above us after piercing the thin layer of life-giving atmosphere. This is also when lonesomeness begins to ring out, in a monotone like the hum of telegraph poles, separateness, isolation, lack of communication with the general movement of biochemistry and electricity on the little crust of sand that is slowly freezing in its imperceptibly slackening course through an unfathomable icy darkness.

After a while I slid my arm over the side and groped on the floor for the volume that lay by my couch. Some book is always on duty by my side like a nurse: an author, that is, a fellow being, an original, a loudmouth or a whiny can't-make-it (like myself), a prattler, a wag, or a pompous demiurge, sometimes even some honest graphomaniac or ready wit who had a *Festschrift* brought out and front-page editorials in honor of his contributions. So somebody always stands vigil over me on the hard floor next to the tangle of radio wiring, the cable of the special little reading lamp, the telephone coil. I get more and more like Staś Dygat as I barricade myself in my den, withdrawing from the world behind a wall of the latest electronics. I replace Dygat on earth, but for whom do I do it? So I let my arm down and blindly seized the book on duty, which was, for some reason, a book of informal essays by Antoni Słonimski. I am being cute, of course, telling you that I don't know why I reached for a book by Antoni. I always reach for his writings when I want to give myself a treat, reward myself for something, do honor to a good hour or a festive occasion. These visits by Antoni with me are brief ones. Antoni was concise, logical, and expressive, hence laconic. Antoni pays me short visits, never approaching any point of boredom or weariness, my appetite is still keen after his departure, while at the same time I feel grateful to him for his intelligence, wit, understanding. I feel something like pride that Antoni doesn't grow old, that he stays continually youthful, and that his opinions, views, and ideals in spite of everything do not age; that is, they weather, possibly, like everything on this earth, but it is a slow, insignificant process, inherent rather in changes of aesthetic formula, as with the evolutionary changes taking place over time in the beauty of a lovely woman.

Having buttered Antoni up no end—a thing he liked a lot—

in my niche

I suddenly recall that early-summer day, sunny, lush, green, when we accompanied Antoni to Laski, where he remained forever in a tiny convent graveyard in the forest. Among young firs, alder bushes, tall forest grass, and little forest wild-flowers, where the red forest ants scurry busily hither and thither.

But before that we had carried Antoni on our shoulders out of Holy Cross Church, three steps from New World Avenue. The church was decorated with white-and-red standards hanging down all the way from the vault, as that center nave was always decorated when a great Pole had died. We, his colleagues and friends, carried him, and I found myself at the head of the casket, because the other, taller ones had shouldered their way to the front, the foot end, to allow themselves to be photographed. So the whole weight of the casket slumped down on me, and I carried my old friend on my very own hump from the bier to the hearse; and the whole way, groaning with exertion, I listened in terror to the creaking of my bones and thought to myself that after all I owed Antoni this effort, and felt proud that I myself, practically unaided, was hauling the great poet as far as the street, a sunny Warsaw street, the very one which Antoni at one time before the war used to walk with his intimates to go to Wróbel's for a dish of tripe.

Then came Laski, a cheerful little cemetery full of birdsong and old nuns, a short observance; someone must have made a speech, but I don't remember, for I was rounding the tree-grown edge of the graveyard, smelling the flowers, listening to the birds, raising my head up to the hot July sky, and rejoicing in the thought that Antoni would feel good and peaceful here by the side of his wife, Janeczka.

But Antoni would not have been Antoni if he hadn't caused some bother to his solemn mourners. He refused to go down. He simply didn't have enough room in the grave. He was bigger than the standard measurements allowed. I knew about this and wasn't in the least surprised that Antoni did not fit the prescribed dimensions.

So a good deal of time went by, while the grave was being enlarged, before Antoni let himself be buried. We slowly separated along forest paths; we may even have stopped in at the Sisters' for tea. We were sad, but at the same time serene. We felt the loss of Antoni, but there was gladness, too, to be leaving him at such a beautiful place. We were a little afraid that we might not get along without Antoni, that it would be harder, but there was also a touch of satisfaction that he was leaving us strengthened and trained in the struggle for imponderable human values.

Everybody measures everybody, compares, appraises. Antoni, too, is placed on a pedestal here, but elsewhere dismissed with an arrogant wave of the hand; still others take a tape measure to him, shake their heads, and say nothing. I don't know whether Antoni belonged to those who are the greatest of our age—nor do I want to know, for I don't care. I know that he weighed and counted in my life, and not mine alone, that he taught me certain rules that were perhaps a little old-fashioned, perhaps a trifle outdated, and in this way somehow strangely relieved me as I was lost and kept getting further lost in my humble grappling with this life—which is too big, too far-flung, too abundant, and probably too weighty for me.

My First Self-Portrait

Gradually I make a clean breast of everything. Day after day I drag out more and more of my sins. But still, at the bottom of this bag, this black sack, some bones remain and rattle, rattle, and won't let me sleep at night. But what sins are there that keep an old man awake? Are there such wrongs among people as would grind up the conscience like termites an old tree trunk?

Perhaps all this is a figment of literature, beginning from legends, apocrypha, parables. There grew and gained credibility a great fairy tale about human conscience, about the sins of men and their ultimate miraculous redemption. But I see everywhere knaves and villains who sleep quietly. Before going to sleep they read a little about crime and punishment, then turn their backs and snore like nobody's business.

I want to confess to everything. My little sins will be redeemed by your great ones. What am I to admit to? How much can you sin in a quiet, narrow-gauge, timid life?

I see an autumn, with remains of the gossamer of Indian summer; a group of boys have started a fire, are baking potatoes. A bit to one side, a little boy trips from foot to foot; he is in an adult's coat which not only covers his heels but trails on the ground after him. Also, someone has wound a kerchief around the little boy's head and tied it in a bow under his chin. To keep him warmer, to keep the wind from blowing at his ears. This little boy, now, is too timid to come closer to the fire. He hangs about the periphery; sometimes one of the older ones treats him to a rude joke, another tosses him an overdone potato.

Yes, this is myself, a silly little portrait, an image of a young orphan that originated only with my Uncle and Aunt Blinstrub; and it was my beloved aunt, unused to children, who had rigged me up like that for my first foray among my mates. I didn't remember this, but my elders tried time and again to recall to my mind that kerchief tied around my chin like an old peasant woman's and that frieze coat dragging on the ground. So often was I treated to the story that this melancholy and disreputable little scene took root in my memory and accompanies me all through life; often in mid-life and even now, close to old age, I have had the feeling that I was stepping in place with a foolish expression on my face and that awful kerchief on my head, tied in a bow under my chin. I feel sure that this is how I must have looked at my high-school entrance exam or when I was to be admitted into the Party, and this is surely how I sometimes strike my indulgent reader: a hairy bumpkin's mug framed in that grotesque kerchief and tapering off into an overlong coat.

There are things one is ashamed of which hold the whip over one all one's life. I have always had a lot of these, and some of them I will not confess to till I die. Perhaps these infamies will pupate into sore, brittle honors, and from those pupae the foul caterpillar ambition will crawl forth in the end.

Aunts of the Revolution

In the fifties Poland was governed by Aunts of the Revolution. Please don't try to correct me. I know it is taught in the schools that authority was exercised by Bierut, Cyrankiewicz, or Różański at that time. But in actual fact we were all irrevocably subject to the Aunts of the Revolution.

They were ladies of middle age, but not yet old, although crones who could remember Lenin could be found among them; not particularly handsome on the whole, though some might be nice-looking and even stake modest claims to masculine attention.

They tended to be on the brunette side, bony, with close-cropped hair, energetic, decisive in their movements, in love with Marxism-Leninism, and fanatically devoted to the People's Rule. For the most part, they came from wealthy Jewish families and had already served a certain apprenticeship in the prewar Communist Party.

Every one of us must have been in touch with one of these

functionaries in his time. They sat in the offices of the Central Committee, in the recesses of the Ministry of Security, in the inspection and approval halls of cinematography, and also in the humble little rooms given to publishing and editing work.

I don't know about others, but I used to feel a sort of refreshing disquiet when I crossed paths with one of these lady comrade directors or editors. I know that a lot of people fled them like the plague, but probably without reason.

You see, I used to find pleasure in the low-key, long-term demoralization of these lady comrades. Their dogmatism, their masculine ways and sexless dispositions acted on me like a red rag on a phlegmatic bull. I don't mean that I charged into battle like Roman Bratny, pardon the comparison, who lured many lady comrades from the path of virtue. A good many provinces could have been populated by the uncompromising female functionaries seduced by this writer.

This wasn't my way; I used a slow corruption, adapted to the mentality of the victim, offering her various earthly temptations, leading her into a permanent state of ideological uncertainty.

Unusual resistance was offered by a certain prominent comrade from the publishing sphere. Since she was no longer suitable for sex and too case-hardened for ideological erosion, a council of war by a number of devoted men resolved to destroy her morally.

So on a certain Saturday, or possibly Sunday, we lured her to a place outside Warsaw under the pretext of a name-day party for one of her employees. And indeed, a black Volga sedan delivered the official personage, who, full of high-principled geniality, entered the tumbledown prewar country house wearing an incorruptible little smile—and if that little smile could have made a sound, it would have rung like steel.

Oh yes, she resisted us, she fought like a lioness, she called to her aid quotations, the authority of our leaders, and harsh memories of the years of struggle. But we had nothing to say; I lay low, I just mooned at her with my honest, trustful Lithuanian eyes and kept refilling her glass. Toast followed toast, now to this, now to that, now to the one who is here, now to the Absent One who watches over and leads us. She couldn't refuse, she couldn't show any weakness to us equivocal types devoid of a clear class affiliation, so with a stiff movement she would seize the crystal beaker, saying: "Well, comrades, bottoms up!"

What followed makes fearful telling. She exchanged kisses and drank *Brüderschaft* with members of former reactionary organizations, she slavered to dance on the tabletop, she hitched up her trousers, which displayed the severe lines of female infantry; but presently turned pale, staggered, and made her way to the shrine of St. Vomitus. Compassionate ladies from her office hove her somewhere outdoors and applied first aid till morning.

And in the morning a different person emerged, a new persona of the female sex. Along with that dreadful night, that odd test of character, there faded into oblivion her doctrinaire spirit, clarion voice, sweeping gestures, and magnificent aptitude in the use of quotations.

A few days later I met on the staircase a pleasant, dapper little brunette who was tearing off, rump wagging, terribly late, frenzy in her eyes, to some briefing to be held for the activists' group. This was our Aunt of the Revolution.

These days they are gone, almost gone. An avalanche of various strange historical events, earthquakes that have shaken the moral sphere, uncertainty that has tainted all given data, all these have dispersed the Aunts of the Revolution, shooed them into mouse holes, and reduced them to wiping their grandchildren's bottoms and boosting them on the swing. Some even sought refuge in churches, of all places, where they rattle off reedy prayers.

Himilsbach and Others

Himilsbach is an ornament of our literature. I have the honor of being friends with this writer. It is not your violent or passionate kind of friendship, but we meet from time to time, render each other small courtesies, and like to take time off for a chat. In the thirty-odd years of our acquaintance Himilsbach has become sedate and white-thatched, and these days he may be seen on Krakowskie Przedmieście or New World Avenue, a living classic being respectfully supported at the elbows by assistants, acolytes, and admirers.

I am not only friends with Himilsbach, I also read his books. In this floodtide of literary barbarism, loutishness, not to mention a most abysmal level of language, with which overachievers and milksops try to floor their readers, i.e., their relations and acquaintances, Himilsbach's prose, spare, clear, I would even say elegant, provides relief by its noble tone and its fine literary manners.

Himilsbach came to literature from the stonemason's calling. At least that's what he maintains, and it wouldn't be proper to doubt his word. Though, to be sure, the impartial observer is somewhat taken aback by the fact that Himilsbach's papers show November 31 as his birth date. Still—a lot of odd things are apt to happen to outstanding people.

Himilsbach, then, was—perhaps still is—a "rough diamond." I make a point of using this term from the film industry because I can't write that he was an amateur. In his field everyone is an amateur. Even Mickiewicz. The writing of verse or prose is an amateur's activity. And any amateur you see wandering the streets may be a celebrated author tomorrow, to be proclaimed a classic in a year or two.

I only mean to say that Himilsbach created or initiated the parade of rough diamonds through our literature. Dygat and I once kibitzed while a good, intelligent fighter, Edward Kurowski, ranked second on the national boxing team; the next time we three met, we were colleagues and the setting was the Writers' Society. Another case I remember was that of a most likable customs officer, Tadeusz Zawierucha, whom we discovered for our literature. He once discovered me at the airport when I was returning from abroad and something like five planes were landing at the same time. I was standing in the lobby, which was jammed full of luggage and, what was worse, incensed passengers trying to battle their way to the customs gate. It was then that I heard the velvety voice of my namesake: "Mr. Konwicki, which would be your suitcase?" He was standing before me in his tunic, and I couldn't think how he had got here. Perhaps he, too, had returned from abroad, or he had got in through some pull to welcome guests of his. However this might be, I showed him my little pilgrim's chest, pretty heavy at that, and he pulled a rubber stamp out of his trouser pocket, breathed into its caoutchouc innards, and with a vigorous movement stamped my luggage.

"Pass on, please," he said.

To me it seemed as if an archangel had intoned the hymn to joy. Joyfully, too, I seized my suitcase and sped home.

I remember Bohdan Hamera, who from a working-class background went through the army and ended up in literature. He, however, kept his distance, although sometimes at meetings he accosted me confidently, as if appealing to shared proletarian origins. Some bricklayers also hung around the society's café.

But I must mention Jan Papuga, mariner and literary man. A real sailor, who all through the war served in the Polish Navy in the West. In the forties, when in Warsaw on business, he very often stayed with me, that is, in my little fourth-floor apartment on Frascati Street. That was the time when Andrzej Braun, too, still in his poetic phase, used to lodge with me. Janek used to turn up in the small hours or at dawn, when the trains from Szczecin arrived.

Papuga was of middle height, but powerfully built, like a true sailor. He talked in an odd, somewhat lisping sort of voice and always about matters of great weight, like his having taken up the cudgels for somebody on his way, wanting to save somebody from injury, having got off the train halfway and being left behind to wait for the next. He also used to report to us on the literary business which brought him to the capital. Everybody here liked him, but he had a hard time getting something published.

At one time he very earnestly started to talk me into a scheme by which the three of us—himself, Franek Gil, a famous reporter of prewar and immediate postwar times, and myself—would rent a house on the Szczecin estuary and start a fishing and writing cooperative. Papuga had many noble and superficially alluring ideas, always rooted in respect and adoration for literature, but nothing ever came of these. Later Janek stopped coming, seemingly lost without a trace; and one day, quietly, without flourish, he betook himself to the other world. But perhaps somebody will yet pick up his earthly trail, some Polonist will start digging in his literary remains, for it would surely be worth it; surely this original mind ought to be preserved for posterity.

Among these authentic rough diamonds there sometimes crept in phony ones. Marek Hłasko proved such a one. He turned up in Warsaw one year, pretending to be a truck driver from Lower Silesia. But he was quickly unmasked. A descendant of belted earls ensconced in the front seats of the Commonwealth Senate of yore, he was unable to sustain his roguish incognito for long. Now and then still another tried some hanky-panky, but quickly withdrew and settled down as a meek ant in the literary heap.

And now there aren't any rough diamonds to be found in these circles. Or one might consider the entire Writers' Society as made up of rough diamonds. Everybody writes these days—generals, pensioners, policemen, priests, fallen women, and angels. All frontiers have been erased. All are writers, and if they aren't, they soon will be.

One time Himilsbach, slightly inebriated, negligibly, in fact, began to demand something from me. I really don't remember today what it was, perhaps an informal loan between colleagues, perhaps my participation in further projected colloquies. I rebuffed him, wanted to get rid of him, did not feel in the mood for banquets. Himilsbach fought me up one side and down the other, grappled with my reluctance, strove to overcome my resistance; till abruptly, as if suddenly broken, he exclaimed in a voice carrying a trace of real tears: "Who gave you the moral right to write about me?"

Who indeed . . . ?

my father's
1919- 1920 service medal

The Flunked Exam

I wake up in the night. I find myself coming to from a daze in the daytime. I suddenly regain consciousness toward evening. Flunked the exam. Come a cropper near the end of life. I had bombed on the exam covering my entire, over half-a-century-long, life.

Exams are the obsession of my vegetable existence here. How many years have I not been taking exams! Scholastic, professional, ideological, moral, character-and-personality ones. My intimates also kept taking some sort of exams, were incessantly subjected to tests and appraisals. I used to dream of exams at night—the only dreams, the only dreams without color. For that matter, all my dreams have been black-and-white.

The final incident of my novel *A Chronicle of Young Love* is a flunked exam, which determines the entire life to come. But what about one's past life? The life that lies behind us?

Everything is collapsing. The whole world around me, before me, behind me, above me, all is cracking, crumbling, sifting, turning to powder, to a pall of dust, to an acrid, opaque cloud which stings and blinds the eyes, smothers the breath, inspires dread, panic fear, horror of horrors.

The Royal Palace downtown was on fire today. There seem to be an awful lot of fires in the world. Here, too, they happened under the Gierek regime; they resembled those mysterious, never explained conflagrations which used to ravage Moscow for months in the nineteenth century, and St. Petersburg, too.

I walk out of the house and go back at once, because something tells me that I left the gas burning or the radio on. Fires, calamities, sudden misfortunes. A sky like the one framing Christ's agony, as painted by the Dutch painters, as seen above the bay of San Francisco. The sky that sometimes seethes overhead with Himalayas of black clouds, among which flash the hues of a sick atmosphere.

Providence favors the Communists. It has long been observed that the only fine day at the beginning of spring is the first of May. Let that day start out ever so dark and dismal, before noon the sun is sure to shine. On May 1 in Warsaw you don't have to carry an umbrella. Providence favors the Communists. Polish ones, at any rate.

It figures that Providence whacked me over the head when I raised my gaunt arm against Communism. From the moment I began to publish my unpleasant little books in improper quantities fate ceased to favor me. And since the proclamation of martial law, my affairs, my business interests, my schemes fell into a catastrophic state. Abruptly everything went dead. Books which were in production abroad suddenly dissolved into fog; others which had barely made it to publication turned out to be hopelessly translated, or were paid no attention or dismissed with disdain. Foreign publishers started cutting me; about the domestic ones silence is best. On the thirteenth of December of the year we all know so well, my death struggle as an artist began. Someone bewitched me. Someone cast a spell on me. Someone pushed a long pin into the belly of a doll representing my anemic person.

The specter of Communism circles over Europe and over Warsaw, which is at the very center of Europe. The specter of Communism gazes at midnight or before dawn into the window of my dwelling, where I snivel quietly as a mouse (do mice snivel?). A repulsive specter, baring its teeth in a sardonic grin.

She

Yesterday I put in a full tank. I began demurely at our club with two vodkas and soda water. These I drank back to back with a suitable interval between first and second. I sipped the stuff gently like medicine, like valerian drops to settle heart and mind. I let my eyes wander lazily about the lounge and failed to spot anybody of interest. That's good, I thought, it's actually better this way. I am going to numb myself with these two gills, only half a pint; I'll drown the worm of care to the point where I can just get myself home and flop down and sleep a quick dreamless sleep till dawn. Modestly I slurped at my potion, but in my middle, somewhere between the larynx and the stomach, something quivered, quaked, vibrated with a joyful unease. I wanted to make it home as soon as possible, cradled by that good little vodka on an empty stomach; I privately swore to myself that I would presently pay and leave, but my eye kept roaming over the nooks of the lounge, poked into the half-murk of the corners, hung on the entrance door. In my heart I knew I was going to let myself go, but good.

And now I come up to the door of my apartment and wait there with a sluggish heartbeat. There is no one at home. Very cleverly I have managed to disperse all the inhabitants. It cost me a good few weeks of intrigues, subterfuges, laborious negotiations. Finally, then, I am alone. And I end up waiting at the door, in the dark passage, since for some unknown reason I am afraid to turn on the light; so with a feeble heartbeat, fogged by the onset of a terrific hangover, I await her coming.

Actually, last night I did end up with a majestic jag. At the tail end of the evening some people I knew and some people they knew began to drop in. Finally a bunch got together who wanted to have a drink with me, and I began to feel like doing maybe a half quart with them, not a lot, not standing on two feet really, because I was anxious to get home, important business coming up tomorrow, only I couldn't tell what.

After that I saw, as in El Greco pictures, in separate frames with outlandish settings, elongated figures of people known to me and unknown; I was aware of sweaty faces greatly drawn out and distorted, with one of them I drank *Brüderschaft*, with another I exchanged kisses, to a third I expressed respect, to a fourth love. I rode somewhere, got out somewhere, was beset by some strange apartments and stairwells and eventually fell into a healthy sleep. I woke up to notice a curtained window before me and outdoors a nice morning full of twittering sparrows and cooing pigeons. What a good thing, I thought to myself, that I got up the energy to return home. Nothing like waking up in your own home when fighting a whopping hangover.

But then a dire premonition assailed me. I looked at the wall near where I was lying. That wasn't my own wall, which I know so well. Some kilim hung on it, and on it a little picture which I wouldn't have hung even on the staircase. Next to the couch stood an unfamiliar little chair with my coat flung over it like a dishrag.

This is the end, I thought in despair, and meant to close my eyes. But a sudden panic jabbed my vitals, an awful dread at the thought of meeting strangers in the morning who were going to tell me what I had been doing all last night, how I had entertained the capital and the outlying regions.

So I began to run, on tiptoe, though not without tottering, around that strange room, trying to complete my toilette. The heart in my chest beat intermittently and with unnatural strength, like a church bell. Only don't let me die in a strange house, I prayed fervently as I pulled on my trousers.

Still on tiptoe, in stocking feet, shoes under my arms, I crept out into the passage and made out the door to the staircase, a door like one belonging to a walk-in safe, lined with sheet iron and armed with a flock of locks European and transoceanic. With shaking fingers I started to take this complex machinery apart, but at the last moment curiosity arrested me on the threshold. Never would I have forgiven myself later if it hadn't; it would have gnawed at me to my dying day. So, again on tiptoe but groping along the walls, I returned to the depth of the passage, where I had seen an open bedroom door, the hosts' bedroom door, if that's who they were. And I saw a couple sleeping like rocks, all unbuttoned on rumpled sheets; she was half naked and her flattened breast, almost masculine in this position, flashed in my sight; right then, though, I bumped against the door, something toppled on the way, and a male voice wailed inquiringly from the bedroom; but I slammed the door behind me and fell head over heels down the tiled stairs, which were marked by an irregular pattern of dog puddles.

Now I am standing in my own corridor, waiting, with my heart beating sluggishly. It must be twelve or more hours since my return home. I had gone to sleep at once, then woken up, unable to sleep anymore, or to live for that matter. Nothing was in working order. My head felt like a stone, eyes dim, breathing stifled, and where my heart used to be, something whimpered hopelessly, as if the dregs were running out of some cracked bottle. I died there for a long time; then I stopped dying and embarked on a cautious revival.

All this I had done for her sake. I had just about killed myself with that vodka out of awe of her. Out of love for her I had risked my life.

It started a year ago. I met her at the pool. Or strictly speaking, I just noticed her as she ambled down the side of the pool at the Legion Sporting Club. I saw a tall girl, no, not a girl, a young woman, taller than I by perhaps half a head, tawny-skinned or already tanned, elegant even in her poolside getup, with some sort of distinction to her that might even be a bit old-fashioned, but also wearing a little gold chain around her left, or perhaps her right, ankle. Her hair was dark, brushed straight back, and gathered into a knot. She had attractive breasts, and they were not too carefully covered, either; also pretty feet. Everything about her was pretty; she might have been a model. Gorgeous, I thought, but not for me. Such young girls are only seen in illustrated weeklies in the company of millionaires, playboys, or handsome gigolo types. Not for me, I thought without real regret, checking in the shower-stall mirror whether anything had changed for the better in my silhouette. What I saw was the usual, though: a not very personable fellow of middle age, a trifle too wide in the hips, and yes, with a tendency to put on weight.

But later, when I stood in the orangeade line, turning this

encounter over in my mind and glad that I didn't have to enter
into complicated relationships with too-high-powered ladies of
luxury like her, and thanking the Lord for leading me not into
temptation, I suddenly saw her cruise helplessly along the other
line. This is how it began.

I offered to help her, bought her a mineral water; together
we went on the lawn where she sunbathed; later I waited at the
ladies' cloakroom, then accompanied her to the bus. That's how
it all began.

I am standing in the dark corridor of my apartment, listening
for her steps. She won't take the elevator, she is afraid of it,
that tight cage from which there is no escape. Every moment,
or perhaps every undetermined time span, I feel the sincere
urge to make a quick getaway, run off somewhere, to the park
or to the movies, some uninteresting film. But I myself wanted
this, after all.

At first I hunted for her in the places where, I discovered
later, she used to go with her husband. Later on, after a month
or two, I became friends with her husband, became his pal,
confidant, friend. What a congenial and useful wimp of a sidekick I was for him! Often he himself pushed me onto the dance
floor. "Go ahead, dance with her," he would say genially, but
with a touch of unpleasant condescension, unpleasant actually
to himself. "Go ahead, dance, she likes you a lot."

I danced, I helped her shop, I wangled my way into receptions
to which they were invited, I visited them and brought presents,
I spent raw evenings camped under her window, under their
windows, I followed them, as if by accident, on their vacations,
I wangled some award for him, helped him to a promotion—
take this with a grain of salt, of course. My point is that I became
a part of their lives, a sort of household fixture. And he thought
. . . I don't know what he thought. He was cordial, patronizing,
friendly.

She, however, said no at every critical moment. When during
a dance I kissed her on the earlobe; on a boat ride, when I
helped her get in and accidently on purpose put my arms around
her breasts. On a long stroll at night—this was when we had
been walking for some time in an amazing sort of eloquent,

telling, lapidary silence—she suddenly stopped and said, "Let's go back." I pleaded for us to go on, and my plea was a proposition, a request, an entreaty for what I had been seeking these many months. And she again whispered, "No."

At the foot of the stairs the door clangs. Someone is summoning the elevator, which rides down to the lobby with a penetrating groan. That's not her. She is afraid of the elevator. The threshold of transgression. The onset of betrayal. Of what had been before, when I wasn't there. Before I had waylaid her by that pool, where swimmers were practicing free-style in two side lanes, and some clown of a coach or official kept playing the same record at increasing speeds.

Yesterday noon she said it: "I can come tomorrow night." "What time?" I asked. "I don't know. I have to play it by ear. Wait for me." Easily said, wait for me. I have been waiting a year or more. Now this hits me like a brick on the head. A soft, delicious brick. Later, though, after we parted, I felt an ache. At which point I decided to resort to the narcotic that has served me since childhood; I went to the appropriate place and ordered two vodkas.

And now the hangover. At times something gives a shudder inside me. Never mind. What do you mean, never mind? I have waited for this evening so many months, after all. How hard and fervently I have worked for this appearance of hers in my house, which I had labored so to evacuate and then adorned like a swan's nest!

And suddenly, without hearing her footsteps, I heard an ever so quiet tap at my door. The sensation nearly knocked me down. I opened the door with shaking hands. "It's you," I said, as if I had really expected someone else.

She gave me a smile that was enigmatic and seemingly without embarrassment. "Please; please," I whispered so quietly that I didn't hear myself. Helplessly I cleared my throat as I closed the door.

She started down the corridor on her own. She was wearing some sort of fancy dress, a bizarre hat, and, I noticed, stockings on her legs, though everyone had been sweltering under a broiling heat since morning. I swear to God, I thought, what a woman! What business do I have with her? Is it possible that she came to me of her own accord?

We sat down in my room, which in the family was known quaintly as the office. She again gave a polite smile, as if she were visiting in a middle-class parlor. "Is it all right to smoke?" she asked. I gave her a light and lit up myself. Behind the window the sun was hiding in a thicket of middling tenements, crooked skyscrapers of a sort. A streak of crimson wandered across the walls. She didn't notice the couch, and I refrained from looking in the direction of that shameless piece of furniture, which for some reason suddenly seemed to be a flowery catafalque.

She crushed her cigarette. "We get undressed, I suppose," she half asserted, half inquired. She got busy taking that costume off. She did it with efficient movements, systematically, not dropping anything on the floor. I tore everything off me with shaking hands. Something popped shyly, and I got entangled for a short while.

But she, with that strange little smile, or perhaps a half smile, naked by now, crossed her outspread hands over her breasts with their all but golden tan and slowly moved to the couch, lay down by the wall, and covered herself with the blanket I had taken away from my son so he wouldn't drag it along to some camp.

Lifting my knees high like a stork and screening with one hand what needs screening, I quickly made my barefoot way to the couch and flopped down next to her. It was getting dark by this time, and in the early dusk her face changed, became a little unfamiliar but perhaps even more beautiful, and all of a sudden the whites of her eyes shone with a silvery gleam.

In silence I began to kiss her face, touching my lips to her eyebrows, nose, mouth with a somewhat premeditated tenderness. She listened to me; sometimes those silver thimbles of her eyes turned my way. So I played off this bit of sentiment as an obligatory prelude and myself wondered what would happen next. Every now and then scraps of cynical thoughts fluttered through my heavy, hung-over head, such as how many times she might have done this before, and what inclined her to take this step, and what would come of it later, when we had become lovers dragging out their stealthy romance over months and years.

Then suddenly, I don't even know when, everything became simple, effortless, as if abetted by Providence. I was already inside her, in this lovely body created by nature for supermen. And I sailed along in a kind of wistful mood, steeped in mild sweetness and heavy languor. A remnant of sobriety signaled to me that she remained passive, that somehow she did not know what everybody knows, or was unwilling, or simply resisting. This being so, I diligently sailed ahead into a gloom lined by residual clarity, a blackness suffused with crimson; I kept tacking against a peculiar tender stubbornness, carrying before me this splendid woman, who with tightly closed eyes remained in an uncanny motionless expectancy. At some point amid the ocean, the pacific ocean, I seemed to notice that she abruptly, almost imperceptibly, stiffened for an instant, as if she had remembered something.

Presently she gasped. I opened astonished eyes and saw her clench her teeth with all her might, while persisting in her silence and immobility, separated from me as if by a wall, a continent, a season.

So I pushed ahead unhurriedly, surprising myself by my calm, courage, and endurance. All this time she lay as in the beginning, inert, taking no part in my blissful labor; some two or perhaps three more times she gasped as if she had touched a hot iron, and two or three times her delicate cheeks paled under their filmy tan.

At length—night had fallen and the sky had merged with the black houses—a moment came when she said in a sleepy and a trifle capricious tone: "I want a cigarette." I, without withdrawing from her, retrieved the cigarettes and matches from the floor by a highly acrobatic feat, twisting like a corkscrew. We both lit up. As I inhaled the smoke, for a moment I saw her face, caressed by a veil-like reddish haze, and a silvery glint from the white of an eye. She seemed a stranger to me; I was taken aback by this, and the enigma of it pleased me strangely.

Later on she whispered she had to phone home. And though

she had never set eyes on this room before, and though it was dark—for only a rectangular reflection from a streetlight lay across the floor—she unhesitatingly leaned over me and lifted the receiver from the phone on the little table by the couch. Unerringly she dialed the number which I knew so well, which I used to dial so often in order to hear her voice, only to panic at once. She dialed that number, waited for somebody to answer at the other end, and began to talk in an entirely neutral voice about various domestic matters—while something like an urge to protest began to grow in me, a distaste, perhaps a twinge of jealousy.

So again I pushed off from the shore and began to swim with round, measured movements. And she, with the receiver at her ear, as if absentmindedly, began to follow my motions, without rebuking me in the least or invoking moderation and decency. And I was gradually seized by a shabby contentment, a base self-satisfaction.

Eventually she replaced the receiver and sank back on the same place on the couch. I fell upon her with a joyous, triumphant violence and knew nothing further until at last I emerged from the awesomely prolonged delight and saw in the darkness her serene face, to which life returned terribly slowly. I bent over her and touched her oddly chapped lips with a very gentle kiss. She returned it with the same tenderness.

Later we lay side by side, smoking cigarettes. She threw off the blanket and lay naked, with shamelessly outspread legs and no constraint about my presence; her breast, with its sharply erect nipple, moved lightly like a white kitten against my throat. I might devour her with my eyes as much as I wanted, while she eyed me from her height with a sort of mild indulgence.

Eventually she got up and, without shielding herself from my glance, went over to the chair to get dressed. As she traversed the rectangle of brightness from the streetlight I saw her brilliantly white, as in a magnesium flash.

Finished with dressing, she came over to the couch, where I lay modestly covered by the blanket, bent over me, and kissed me with lips that felt hot. "Don't bother to see me out," she said quietly, "I'll find my way. Farewell." I was taken aback to hear her say "Farewell."

The following month was similar to those preceding. But it offered no more occasions for intimate meetings. Accordingly, what was left was those surreptitious kisses while dancing or on long walks, secret holding of hands at the movies or under the tablecloth at supper, and that thrill of communion between eyes which would pierce you all of a sudden when it was least expected.

At last there occurred that next occasion I had long looked forward to. We were in a pub somewhere with other people, without her husband, who had stayed at home for some urgent work. We came out onto the street in the middle of the night, and it so happened that we came out even pairs. And I could take her away, drive her wherever I wanted, snatch her from that street under the cloak of legality. But when I took her arm so tenderly, with such an inner tremor, such an abrupt rush of feelings, she suddenly said in a sober, matter-of-fact voice: "Go away." "What does that mean?" I stammered, flabbergasted. "Off you go," she added.

I let go of her hand and went off into a side street, thrust on by wounded ambition, lacerated honor, the presentiment of yet another breakdown in life. And she joined the other people again, for she wanted to stay there and get rid of me; and I caught the sound of her laugh, which I knew so well, and which I will remember all my life, all the same.

But did I at some time experience this, or did I simply note down a literary idea for some story or book? Where does memory end and fictional routine begin? It doesn't matter. Or rather, it is all a sport of the imagination, natural or drugged. It doesn't matter.

Brief Stroll down New World Avenue

It's really true, New World Avenue in bird's-eye view or, properly speaking, seen from a plane, looks like a curved Turkish saber. I corrected myself because we don't know, after all, what birds see. So I have no business calling on flying poultry; better rely on the impressions of fellow mammalian bipeds.

New World Avenue is not a long street. From Świętokrzyska Street to Aleje Jerozolimskie it is six hundred, perhaps seven hundred yards long (I pretend ignorance in order to mobilize the encyclopedists among my readers). Past Aleje Jerozolimskie, New World Avenue runs on some hundred fifty yards before merging into Three Crosses Square.

The true New World Avenue was the prewar one. Crowded with life, abuzz with pedestrians, abounding with famous shops, cafés, restaurants, and cinemas. After the war, New World Avenue at first acquired dignity, for it was rebuilt just as it had once been—untainted by commercialism and trash, in the style of the little eighteenth- and nineteenth-century palaces. It looked like a museum and it was bleak like museums: a few shops, a few cafés, a few offices. The stateliness, however decked out with color plaster, stucco, copper sheeting, and antique tile, exacted a high price from the inhabitants. It was a pretty little artery, but on the empty side.

Later New World Avenue began to lose its looks. Plaster and cornice work started to fall off (I saw a man killed by a chunk of cornice from a balcony), eaves turned black, roof tiles cracked, display windows crusted over with grime—but more and more life burgeoned on it, a bit indiscriminate and vulgar perhaps, but life, after all. Café bars sprang up, bistros of sorts, the network of streets was reanimated, above all Chmielna Street (now running under some new label, of course), the stronghold of private enterprise, which bails out the ideologically correct but sluggish government in the matter of productive and commercial initiative.

On the other hand, this scrubby New World Avenue, falling apart from neglect and refurbished skin-deep and reviving anew, will never again attain that prewar vivacity which was described and graphically demonstrated, during strolls that were improvised causeries, by my beloved mentor and friend, Henryk Tomaszewski, the prominent graphic artist and emblematic figure of the artistic world of Warsaw in the postwar years. Henryk lived on New World Avenue for a long time, on the stretch which to me is the inferior one between Aleje Jerozolimskie and Three Crosses Square. He occupied a roomy and very charming studio loft, like a bachelor flat but well appointed, where you could always pick up a drink or a snack. A notorious feature was the "scrambled eggs" one might enjoy at Henio's in the small hours after an exhausting carousal about town. It goes without saying that these scrambled eggs were elitist in character, the exclusive prerogative of those whom Henryk liked; and he had always been rather fastidious in the matter of friends. Anyone who proved not to his liking was apt to receive a label that might stick to him for decades.

The way it has come out, the above makes it seem that the Henio of his New World Avenue epoch—he hasn't been living there for years now—was a supercilious loudmouth who looked down upon people. But this is far from the truth. Henryk was and is one of the most charming and good-natured persons I have met in my life. All I meant to suggest is that he is no hail-fellow-well-met softie into whose apartment any jackass might blunder.

I had the honor of being Henryk's companion for a long time, at banquets, at work, even on vacations. Henryk taught me the Warsaw of prewar student days, Warsaw streets, Warsaw customs, pubs, and theaters. Beyond this, Henio taught me something of life. I mean, not perhaps life as such, for I was no spring chicken anymore and had seen a bit of life myself. Henio taught me the aspect of life that has to do with the rigors and demands of art. He shared with me his artistic as well as his psychological experience. For like every artist, Henryk was, and is to this day, an unfulfilled actor, director, writer, or, to put it simply, a penetrating observer of the great human family.

Well—suddenly it turns out that I am writing a catalogue introduction for him or a stray paragraph of appreciation, when all I had in mind was a short stroll along New World Avenue arm in arm with the gentle reader. On the other hand, there is no way one could bring off such a promenade without encountering Henryk, who, though he now lives far from midtown, is present here in spirit; and as long as the Melody Tavern will yet pluck upstanding or bedraggled customers out of the night,

view from my balcony

so will our spirits, that is Henryk's and mine, wheel in sprightly rounds hither and thither on New World Avenue at midnight.

This street, modest and shortish yet so momentous to Warsaw, witnessed many important postwar events. Starting from various disorders and riots (your pardon, Mr. Censor) when, treated to nightsticks and whiffs of tear gas, we scrambled through courtyards to the hinterland of this artery, and on to respectable and outright historical happenings like the passage of presidents, first secretaries, and Pope John Paul II. Needless to say, as a notorious and passionate gaper I did not miss any occasion—and I have lived here almost thirty years, after all. So I may have seen in the shallow canyon of this street Nixon as well as Carter, though I am not sure of that, but with absolute certainty I have seen the famous Nikita Khrushchev and the torpid dignity of Brezhnev. The Pope blessed everybody as he passed through this street, so I, too, was vouchsafed a portion of this blessing.

I live in a rear apartment off said street, which would make it difficult to watch the passage of these pageants. But my father-in-law, Alfred Lenica, a waterproof (i.e., oil) painter, as Henio would call him, lived on New World Avenue in the building that has a shop with musical instruments on the bottom floor. Hence it was from the studio of Alfred, my dear father-in-law and ever improving painter, whose pictures do better and better although he has been dead seven years, that I lay in wait for all such solemnities, as well as home-and-garden clubbings of anti-government demonstrators (apologizing to Mr. Censor, once again).

This building where Alfred lived, while very quiet and upper-class, had a fairly unrestful neighborhood. This is the spot in Warsaw where most mysterious fires break out. My frail memory retains a fire on the roof of the big delicatessen, something burning in Alfred's building itself, and a blaze in the loft next door. That makes three fires in the space of ten to fifteen years. Near my own place, by contrast, gas explosions predominate. Several neighborhood apartments have already gone up in the air. No wonder that when I leave home I go back seven or eight times to check if something is not burning, glowing, or blazing.

Our beloved New World Avenue ages with terrible rapidity. Some splatter artists or brick flippers have hardly given it a face-lift when it is already decrepit again and on its last gasp. By this time the city fathers have given up on this street altogether. When the Pope was coming, they cunningly slapped some oil paint over the first-floor walls, just what the foreign TV cameras would see.

This being so, I drag myself from the paillasse in my niche—guard post of eternal vigilance—and stride forth on a vesper stroll along New World Avenue and vicinity while it is still alive; while we are still alive.

My Faith

A sunny Sunday in early summer. I am back from a walk. Dusk is slowly falling. It comes from the east, perhaps actually from

Wilno or Nowa Wilejka. In a sweeping drape of cold it bears the fragrance of gillyflower and the monotonous buzz of the cockchafer, which haven't been with me for so many years. I feel weak, as I do every Sunday. For some time now I have been conducting myself in an exemplary fashion, and the sight of me with a shot glass in my hand is a genuine rarity. And yet I continue to have a slight hangover on Sunday. Not a dinosaur, not a dragon, not a man-eater, as I used to have, but the kind of mildly snappish hangover that attends gentlemen of mature years. I really haven't any idea where it comes from, or how it happens that it is always on that misbegotten Saturday that I sneak a little glass or two somewhere. It probably fixed in my genetic code by my artisan or outright proletarian pedigree that after work on Saturday afternoon, washed up and changed into a white shirt, I have to join my shopmates in pouring a little "nip" or "jigger" down the old hatch, or a "double neat," as we now say.

I am listening to the sparrows as they warn off with their screeches the cat Ivan, who is sitting on the hot tin parapet, eyeing me and the room we share through the window, as if gazing into a different world, or perhaps into the other world. So, with his belly full, he is sitting there on the window ledge in the great green basket of the balcony, where some creepers planted by Danka before her trip to see Marysia curl around the wrought-iron rails; there sits old Ivan, pretending not to hear the racket, so exquisitely offensive to his feline ears, of the sparrows minding their little eggs or chicks tucked away in the tree under the balcony, the tree whose name I don't know (encyclopediast readers, here is your chance).

But I, listening to all this happening before a pretty scorching summer evening, have it suddenly come home to me that I haven't heard the church bells for years. This is the time of the Angelus, the prayer about the Lord's Angel, and not one church in Warsaw tolls a bell, as custom demands.

The time I hear bells is on radio programs, TV shows, or in the movies. How many times haven't I myself used the sound of bells in my films! In the sound archives of studios you may find a lot of my bells, not to mention a certain cuckoo from my film *All Souls'*, which to this day knocks about Polish films, even in autumnal scenes.

Bells are my favorite music. I exaggerate, of course, this obviously is only part of the truth, and I don't like it myself when someone asserts that he likes something "best of all." To love but one book, only one film or one symphony, argues a sad deprivation, a deplorable intellectual penury, an unfortunate spiritual narrowness.

Why have the church bells stopped ringing? There probably is some rational cause which I don't know and don't want to know. I prefer to think that this Sunday the bell ringers have simply forgotten to call the faithful to pray for the long dead and for those dying now.

I procrastinate, I hedge, I digress, because I am afraid of the plan I have decided upon after much hesitation, perplexity, and petty inner struggles. I want to, I really must at last, when all is said and done, mention my faith, my religion, and my God. I have to carry this out, I feel an overpowering command to which I wish to submit in order to obtain absolution, exoneration. Peace of mind, or peace of spirit.

We live in times when the chief religions have come to be much alike and have ceased to hate and battle each other. All religions honor a single God, creator of men, earth, and universe. All religions prostrate themselves before a Supreme Power, before all-embracing Reason, before Providence.

And I, wretched worm, who have appeared for a few decades in a small corner of the cosmos, I, too, worship God by my lights in the Roman Catholic Church. Even when I used to return from Party meetings, I would pray before going to sleep, sometimes fervently, sometimes halfheartedly and hastily.

At times I have searched and analyzed myself, suspecting in this need for daily prayer a sort of secret opportunism, a shabby reinsurance, a little candle lighted to a hypothetical God, just in case. But it wasn't that; I don't think it was. And at times, when I was reckless and puffed up with pride, and when a frenzy of protest, defiance, total anarchy seized me, still mornings and evenings, when all human beings of all creeds in the world humbly bend their knees, miserable I, too, would trace on my sinful brow, on my sinful heart, on my sinful shoulder the sign of the holy cross.

It is also true, though, that a thousand times, both day and night, doubts have crept up from all sides: some movement of the gray cells, an intellectual habit of rationalizing self and environment, a hankering to reconcile feeling and reason.

I was terribly anxious to believe and kept losing faith. Perhaps I wished to believe for the sake of inner peace, for comfort, but often also for the sake of God, for His unfathomable greatness, His beauty, His divine godhead. I wanted to believe as everybody does, but couldn't. I wanted to believe at least like humble countrywomen, and couldn't do it.

The mercy of faith. The mercy of faith—and at once there swarm up a million sinful thoughts, acts of sacrilegious defiance, blasphemous doubts. Catholic doctrine, philosophy, liturgy, antiphons, and prayers: how I wish I could enter that world and move in it with the fullness of freedom, confidence, unequivocal thoughts.

I believe and I disbelieve. I am close to the holy and suddenly fall into the dreadful void of unbelief. My road to God is long and all cluttered with the edifices of churches, monasteries, episcopal palaces. And that great tower of Babel of intermediacy, that enormous apparatus of liaison with the Lord, that rushing spate of holiness and bureaucracy, all this discourages and repels me and gives rise to mad complexes.

I realize that in talking of these petty and trivial afflictions of mine I brush up against sin, and I see the penitent's scourge raised over me. But the world rushes along helter-skelter, and so do I. We know more and more, and become aware of more and more complexities. This world is entering a new Red Sea of uncertainty, violent reorientations, abrupt revelations of a restless science. I want so badly to believe but am incapable of steady faith because of the questions and doubts crawling forth from everywhere, and a chronic, ever-present despair.

In any situation I shall always see myself from all sides at once. I shall always be faithful and faithless, good and bad. I shall thirst for holiness and may never come close to it. That is the way I am and the way I may remain to the end, to the finish of my pilgrimage on this earth, which once was the one exceptional miracle performed for the Lord's creatures but by now may be one of many planets inhabited, by the grace of the Creator, by uncounted multitudes of God's races. This is what I may be to the end, although I would like to change, and pray for this change—so that like my mother I might believe strongly, unyieldingly, and to the last moment of this earthly life.

Whenever I enter a church for Holy Mass and hear the sermon, I am seized by a pang of sudden disbelief. That's how it is, it is frightening to talk about, but God, the God who dwells above us, about us, and within us, the Terrible God, the Relentless God, yet at the same time the God who is our sole hope, the sole meaning of our existence—this only recourse of ours invariably withdraws from me in the shadow of the pulpit, faced with the intermediacy of priests, clerics, monks, those, in a way, reverend persons, but still something like officials or functionaries; and I fall into a deep chasm of unbelief and revulsion. How many times have I come out of church all covered with sinfulness, despondency, an obscure terror, wrapped in a fine web of evil thoughts like the floating gossamer of Indian summer.

I want to believe, and I am going to fight to attain my faith. I'll fight by myself or together with those close to me. I daily stand before God the way I am. I have made the day yield as much as I could. I bend my knee before my God with all the sincerity I am capable of. I begin to whisper my daily prayer as just the person I was created by the All-Highest Will.

I believe and I disbelieve. In a turmoil of prayers and curses. In the blaze of annihilation and in the sudden radiance of human saintliness. Amid the priests and charlatans of all religions and all fraudulent sanctuaries. I approach and retreat. And perhaps I shall succeed in an ultimate lucid moment in discerning the greatest truth and merging with it forever.

And if I don't succeed? If I sink into the earth as an ordinary mindless worm?

Falling

Behind the treetops full of juicy young leaves some dreadful
avian tragedy is taking place. I can't make it out because of those
trees; I walk from window to window, shaken by the echoes of
this drama and trying to discover the site of what must be a
disaster. Beyond the green smudge of foliage there is a flicker
of cornice and eave, above that the tiled roof and a mansard
window; and near that window two dark birds are fluttering in
the air with an uncanny wailing noise—perhaps parents crazed
by agony. They will sink to the window level, tussle in the drain
for a moment, and fly a little way up again. One of them perches
on a branch for a moment, only to take off again as if remembering its misfortune. This crying of birds that I cannot make
out so strangely recalls the lament of people wronged. These
birds are in despair like humans and cannot calm down; and I
can't calm down either, and scurry about the house numbed by
this microtragedy and ask myself with my own personal despair
why these poor animals, too, have to suffer, although they have
no part in that game with the Lord, and no Last Judgment or
hell or heaven await them.

   Falling. I took this title from the poem by Tadeusz Różewicz,
a poem which impressed me at the time, and not only me; I
used fragments of it in *Salto*, with the author's permission, just
as on another occasion I inserted among the credits for *The Last
Day of Summer* a passage from another verse. This "falling," that
is real falling itself and the aura of that poetry, has been accom-
panying me for years. I am constantly falling, ceaselessly falling,
as though spurred by Różewicz, and I fall unevenly, now faster,
now more slowly. And this falling movement of late years has
become almost indiscernible, which is why I think more and
more often that I have stopped falling, have come to a halt for
ages in a state of motionlessness; that this is, for that matter,
the end of electric pulsation, the coda of extinct chemical
processes.

   As early as the tag end of Gierek's tenure I began to feel that

I was not alive. I ate breakfast, went out for walks, returned home, had a bite of lunch, thought of various things as I lay in my niche, but my thinking seemed to go on in a fog; then came another walk and afterward the turning from side to side at night, and the same thing next day.

I suddenly became aware at that time that people, too, took me for dead. I wasn't mentioned in the papers, did not appear in public places, and many of the readers who used to cast a glance at my spavined prose thought that I had quietly, discreetly, so as to avoid any fuss, shuffled off this mortal coil; i.e., died. This attitude rubbed off on me somehow, and I toddled along in the shade, on the sidelines, anonymously, with a mild and mellow feeling that I was the late lamented, that all was behind me by now, good and bad, that I was free and, as in those tall tales about life after death, floating in the air and seeing my body stand in lines, push along to a café, or being abused by an angry wife.

And now again, after a number of years, freed by external circumstances from many temptations, I am floundering without any progress through swathes of murk, blundering disembodied in unending night, waiting for that light at the end of the tunnel.

But this time, I am afraid, my beloved readers don't think anymore that I have died and passed to life everlasting. Now, I am afraid, they don't think of me at all, having a lot of other matters to give thought to. Being reckoned dead is better, considering, than being passed over. So I am sinking without falling—perhaps I have been snagged on some cornice and am hanging between heaven and earth, slowly drying up, unnoticed by anyone, like a fly or moth.

All of a sudden the finale of Borejsza comes to my mind. Or perhaps one of a chain of finales. He had been through that dreadful car accident by that time, was ailing and well into the process of falling. He was still busy with the journal *Rebirth* but had already lost control of the Czytelnik concern and was a simple apparatchik, occupying the position of deputy director of the Central Committee's Department of Culture. Thus Anka Baranowska, editorial secretary at the time, and I found ourselves once, perhaps several times, in that former building of the Central Committee's on Chopin Street and were admitted to Borejsza's office, where we were unable to detect many signs of work. And Borejsza was no longer the old Borejsza who took the journal away from Kuryluk by force; we had before us a punch-drunk man who with a naïve defiance held on to the remnants of his authority, prestige, and personal honor.

And on that occasion, when we had completed our business, Borejsza asked meaningly: "You want some Belvederes?" These were a deluxe brand of cigarettes newly released for the narrow market of the higher echelons of Party and government and not yet available to ordinary mortals at the time. We expressed eager interest to the chief; he walked off, falling but pretending otherwise.

With ponderous steps Borejsza approached an enormous black cabinet, an imitation of a Danzig cupboard or perhaps even the real thing, and opened one section of the door. We could see on a shelf a stack of white cigarette packs. Borejsza, shielded from us by his back, took out one pack each for us and was about to return when he changed his mind and put one pack back on the shelf. He took one step in our direction, but then stopped, with clumsy fingers unsealed the pack, and grabbed a bunch of those splendid cigarettes. Then he dropped a few into our palms, as one used to do to the wagon drivers on one's estate.

To think that this man a few years ago made or broke editors of papers and managers of printing houses, nominated ambassadors, and when need arose gave the highest value at every point in time or place—in a word, gave freedom to men enslaved!

Buried in Rubble

In the winter of 1945–46 I traveled with some pals to Katowice, or perhaps to Zabrze or Bytom. We were just excursioning into the nearby country during the university holidays, into the smog-filled world of Silesia. At this point I can't recall the cir-

Uncle Blinstrub   my father

cumstances of that tour, why we were going and whom we were going to see. I only know that one of us, Wiesio or Zdzisio, or maybe someone quite different, was taking us to visit his family.

All I remember is an inhospitable cloudy sky, the cross of a window frame, a bed or couch, and on it, as if on a battlefield, my worn-out self and an ill-used Renia, Tećka, or most likely Lila. I don't remember what led up to this, how it happened that I waged a fierce struggle with that wisp of a girl who was a year or perhaps two years older than I.

This contest began early that evening and in mutual sympathy. Renia or Lila (attractive girls had this sort of name at the time) was a thin, pretty, strangely pale girl with an aura of kindness, tenderness, and discreet intelligence about her. So many years have passed, but I still see her on that humble bed, delicate, tender, and worried. For I was nineteen and after just one thing. I had a lot of strength and tenacity and even more curiosity about sin. I explored that slender body like some marvelous continent, far-off dream island, star from the depths of eternal darkness. Breathless, in a sweat, deaf to the world in the rush of my blood and my hammering pulse, I struggled with this strange girl, who would have surrendered anything to me except the one thing I was after.

I don't know if she remembers me, assuming that she survived everything in between and now lives surrounded by a flock of grandchildren. For I really love her even to this day, the way she stayed in my mind, dark-haired, alarmingly pale, at a loss, and unyielding.

That winter night had many hours, and in all those hours there wasn't a moment's respite. It would seem that she would relent, would have to yield to my persistence, would tire and give up; and there would happen what ought to happen between a boy and a girl when they love each other and want to plunge for the first time into that sweet and thrilling mystery. But at the last moment she always pushed me away, thrust me off, barricaded herself with arms and legs, repeating with the utmost conviction, "Don't, you mustn't, it will make you ill, you'll have a headache tomorrow, it's not right, you'll be tired; sleep, or something bad is going to happen to you."

She repeated this so impressively, adjuring me with tears in her voice, and she breathed such an extraordinary strength of conviction from a fund of hidden experience that I began to soften, after all; a fear of unknown consequences cooled my fervor and weakened my onslaught. The terrible red glow in my eyes faded, and I saw the window again and the Silesian sky behind it.

When she tried to go to sleep, reassured by my temporary passivity, I flung myself on her again in a sudden onrush of desire. And again she reasoned with me earnestly and tearfully, resolutely and with all her heart, about the dangers my designs posed to my health.

And that was how it ended. In terrible exhaustion, a sense of futility and embarrassment, and in the murky dawn of the next day. At length I surrendered. She went to sleep, while I, wakeful, kept my eyes on her pale face with its darkly shadowed eyes and a fine strand of hair that trembled over the eye cavity, agitated by her almost insensible breathing. I never met her again in my life.

There is nothing striking or intriguing in this little story. And yet I forever remember, and constantly find my mind returning to, this trifling episode of forty years ago. What did that girl defend, what did she want to forestall, why did she reject my fervent, boundless puppy love?

She brought off some sort of victory at the threshold of an era which has degraded love to general copulation, the cheapest and simplest entertainment for the broad masses of youth both of the monied classes and from the wrong side of the tracks. She begrudged me a nickel on the eve of the devaluation of millions.

Renia, Tećka, or Lila. A girl from the era buried under the rubble of the last war—the greatest moral catastrophe of modern times.

The Mailbox

I am turning from the courtyard into the stairway of my apartment house—mine for life, mine until the approaching end, my, our, your apartment house. Actually, I creep up to this murky stairwell that smells of urine; if I weren't embarrassed I'd go down on my knees and crawl inside. The thing is, I am peeking (no fair), provoking fate, kicking against the traces of my personal Providence.

And immediately I notice that there is something. For the first time in many days. Behind the rusty slot something shows white, like a bashful glint of underwear. I am not in a hurry, though. I go into low gear, I approach with small steps without looking at the portent, at the arcane repository of my destiny, that Pandora's box of my daily life. I have time, something is in the bag, and it isn't going to run away. Thus I delay as much as possible my ineluctable meeting with the mailbox.

At length, after much fuss with the keys, I open the lid, and onto my outspread hands from the horn of plenty pour the gifts of the contemporary world. Unheard of—four items at one go! My correspondence for the year.

I gallop up the stairs and into the apartment. I administer a slight kick to the shaggy belly of the cat Ivan, who has chosen the wrong time for welcoming ceremonies, and fly into a room where there is more space and more light. With shaking fingers

I open the first letter. Some bore who in a fit of schizophrenia conceived the illusion that he was the editor of a monthly wants me to contribute an article and demands an early reply. The poor fish doesn't know that he'd better not solicit any work from me, for that way trouble lies. I put the offer aside. The cat Ivan instantly plumps down on the letter like a rubber stamp. The cat wishes me well, he thinks I am in for a good thing.

I reach for the second envelope. A lady who would rather not bother to go to an office in a personal matter asks me to do it for her. With a keening growl I put the letter down next to Ivan. But he is way ahead of me. With a contemptuous flick of his tail he whisks the perfumed sheet away. I take up the third item, a heavy-grade envelope, abundantly filled. But I am seized by a sudden aversion. Hesitant and fumbling, I wrench the flap off the envelope. Some devout sisterhood calls on me to join them in prayer at a designated hour.

A dry sob wrenches my bloodless throat. This is my correspondence for the month; these are my links with this world, which is loved by so many people, who claim from me the same kind of love, pleasant optimism, energetic acclaim.

I am holding the fourth letter in my trembling old man's hands. But this lulu I won't even open. In a minute I will get up—let me just gather a little strength—go to the trash can, tear this bit of junk into little pieces, and throw it out. That will be my revenge and a demonstration of pride, an act of defiance toward fate, a challenge thrown to the demons of chance, the idols of chaos, the devils of total senselessness.

I am beset by defectives, dullards, and lunatics. And I haven't heard from the Rockefellers, the King of Sweden, or Prince Rainier in an age.

I feel awfully like talking about Janek Świderski, today a fixed star of the Polish stage, who like everybody else was a young man once, a young actor; and I made friends with him, and we spent a lot of time together, and as happens to everyone, a few little adventures came our way.

I met Janek right after his move from Łódź to Warsaw. If I recall, he was playing the Baron in Gorky's *Lower Depths*. In this part he instantly enslaved Warsaw, and his enactment of it was discussed, recollected, cited in the almanacs of theater for many years.

Before I knew him, when I used to see him sometimes in Polish films, I always thought to myself that here was a fellow who really had the makings of a young Hollywood heartthrob. But, O wonder, Świderski ignored his surface assets, neglected his potential as a great lover on the silver screen, and resolutely strode on toward the representation of character.

Here I find myself counting and cross-checking in order to decide how old Janek was when he elaborated, fashioned, and created that role of the Baron. I would say he was thirty-some. From that time on, he probably always concocted a face for every performance, pasting on, painting, here enlarging, there reducing, in order to conceal himself, hide, disappear behind the mask, behind an invented, or rather created, reality.

I consider this a rewarding case in point for future psychologists of creativity, analysts of the theater of the second half of the twentieth century, sociologists of the acting profession. Anyway, Janek, instead of playing great lovers whose photographic likenesses hang over the beds of young ladies, took the difficult and often thankless road of the character repertoire.

But what I meant to talk about was the youthful Janek and a certain vacation we spent together when we lived in the port city of Gdynia. At that time I tried in relation to Janek to play the part of the marriage broker in Gogol's play *The Marriage*, and Janek in some odd way found himself in the role of Podkolyosin, the reluctant groom. I was pimping and prodding him toward a certain pretty and engaging young lady working in film, for I had been seized by the gambling fever. Janek simply offered resistance, and what was worse, the maddening resistance of Podkolyosin. Whenever I had him launched on a date, he was back after half an hour; every time I tried to leave him tête-à-tête with her, he came running after me; let me set him straight about the sweetness of marital infidelity and the delights of affairs, and he went for his rod, ready to go fishing.

Once, on the margin of my campaign and his dodging, we found ourselves in the Grand Hotel at Sopot or, more exactly, we didn't "find ourselves" but pretty regularly frequented at eventide this shrine of luxury and dissipation, which also was thirty years younger at the time and served patrons more zealously than it does now.

One night, then, we were returning from Sopot to Gdynia. At the time the two places were connected by a roadway paved with cobblestones. It must have been about three in the morning, day was already dawning, but we had also run into one of those sudden nocturnal showers, and we were driving Janek's car, known as a cardboard DKW, a G.D.R. product very popular at the time. This was an archaic species of two-stroke engine encased in a flamboyant plywood shell. The automobile was new and by contemporary standards could pass for elegant, and we were nonchalant and on the loose, the playboy types of the era just after Stalin.

So we bowled along that famous road, talking about life, and Janek let me have various useful hints and lessons, for he was a little older than I and had started on life before the war.

We were just entering Orłow when we saw before us in the haze of the shower an intersection, a trolley-bus stop, and the first bunch of sleepy passengers waiting for the bus.

At this juncture Janek addressed me as follows: "You know, Tadzio, I am such a conscientious driver that whenever conditions are poor, or when there is a drizzle, or when approaching an intersection and seeing pedestrians at a bus stop, I gently apply the brake. Like this, watch."

Here he depressed the brake pedal to demonstrate his circumspection, an action which set in motion a protracted and bewildering episode in my life. The costly new machine produced in the fraternal republic next door began to behave like a wild mustang. It jumped in the air, kicked out in all directions, and started a terribly prolonged, continuous rotation about its vertical axis as it slid on the wet paving stones, at very long intervals hitting whatever was in the way with its rear, flank, or one of its headlights. I had time to say a Lord's Prayer, a Hail Mary, and a Grant Us, Lord, Eternal Rest before we rammed the city transit's cast-iron utility pole with our trunk and came to a complete stop.

We crawled out. Terrified pedestrians stared at us from their shelter, and Janek gave vent to long strings of very ugly words punctuated by groans. He uttered these really indecent formulations and locutions at an oddly retarded tempo, meanwhile bending over and crouching to assess the consequences of our road accident. I writhed and moaned with laughter and fell on the grass strip beside the track; everything was so extraordinary: the hour, the car rearing on its haunches, the sleepy people, and the really enraged Janek.

But Providence watched over us. We had taken that final decisive impact with our spare tire, which in the DKW was mounted on the trunk, so the damage proved moderate.

I am able to recall many other incidents, a great variety of meetings, banquets, hours spent together chatting about life and art, but for some reason the dearest memories seem those of long-ago holidays in a time when the world was sunnier and greener in the summertime and before us lay a whole unknown future, mysterious and alluring. We swished about in that DKW as in a Rolls-Royce, accosted girls behind the back of Murka, whom we used to visit on the beach near Gdynia, playing young virtuous and overworked artists; now and then we had a drink, for courage, other times we played volleyball, or we halted high on the seashore and looked at the gray horizon before us, at the foaming waves and the far reaches of the sea, which roared like a vast water mill and stirred painful longings.

And how could one fail here to visit for a while with Gucieńko, that is Gustaw Holoubek, whom Dygat at one point dubbed Gucieńko; though it's a cinch that the name was invented by Dygat's wife, Kalina Jędrusik. In this playful form of the name, not the most common in the Polish calendar, or rather on Polish birth certificates, an anachronistic tenderness is contained, a touch of old-fashioned elegance, the exotic intimate world of a person on his way God knows whence, God knows whither.

Gucieńko and I actually have more things in common. We come from opposite ends of Poland, but we both had relatively old fathers who early died on us, and we both were children of our mothers' second marriages. If you took a closer look at our pedigrees and also the circumstances we lived in in childhood and youth, you could tell a thing or two about our further fates and hypothesize finales.

Gucieńko thus is almost my brother, and I am a brother to him, and it is with strong emotion that I experience the moment when he steps out of the wings and with a first enigmatic gaze sweeps the audience and myself, who is hidden in it behind somebody's back.

We know all about him as an actor and about his stormy life. Yet a curtain of secrecy covers many of his lesser actions that no one would have associated with him. Gucieńko is a mild, accommodating sort of person, not especially conflict-prone. But as always in such cases, his delicacy has its limits. The virtues I have mentioned grace Gucio up to a point, but after that his other nature, the street gorilla, takes over, that is, the social manners and ethical code he carried over from Cracow's Animal Park. Nobody needs an explanation what these are.

An illustration. Gucieńko, Dygat, another fan, and I are seated in the bleachers of Legion Stadium, in pleasurable expectancy of the start of a soccer match. But behind us on a higher tier a squad of Warsaw rowdies comes to roost. Unmindful of the fact that respectable connoisseurs of the game are sitting in front of them, this gang starts making a racket, tossing some powerful language about, scuffling, whistling, hollering.

Gucieńko, distinguished in his short overcoat, turns around and politely admonishes the young people, pleading for silence. Fat chance! The hooting and hollering, the unedifying vocabulary reach a new level. Gucieńko listens to this, his stately ears flush ominously; suddenly he does a lightning turnabout, grabs the most active hood by the head, whisks it down past his arms, and hammers it, snoot first, against his knee. Lord of Hosts, the entire grandstand goes dead, the hooligans sit in frozen terror, the rowdy grabbed by cunning Gucieńko picks himself up, his nose scrambled; and at this point their leader, a big, burly hulk, rises from the bleacher and announces with distaste: "Let's go somewhere else; this is gangland."

* * *

At some point, at some juncture of history, Jerzy Kawalerowicz
dropped out of my life. He was my partner in running the Kadr
production unit, which created the so-called Polish school of
film, and I also joined him in writing the books of what probably
were his best films; I am thinking of *Mother Joan of the Angels,
Pharaoh, The Inn*. As for his *Night Train*, I also had my crooked
hand in that at the scene-writing stage.

I wasn't a partner in Kadr, properly speaking. Kawalerowicz
was my boss and artistic director, our friend Ludwik Hagar was
the producer, and I was in charge of literary angles. If a film
produced by our unit was a success, later at the official screening
Jurek, gathering the kudos, would say, "Oh yes, in my unit,
Your Excellency . . . ," "For I in directing the unit . . . ," "You
see, I require, Your Excellency . . . ," "Because I am the one
who takes the risks . . ."

But if we bombed, and the official screening produced rockets and dressings-down, Jerzy would say modestly, "Konwicki
and I, Your Excellency . . . ," "For in Konwicki's outfit and
mine . . . ," "You see, taking the risks along with Konwicki . . ."
On these infrequent occasions I luxuriated in togetherness and
was an equal partner.

As you see, Jerzy was, is, and perhaps will remain a hardened
egocentric. For instance, whenever we drove somewhere and
he got out of the car first, I took great care to extend a foot to
catch the brunt of the door he would absentmindedly slam. For
Jurek the process of alighting from a car ended when he had
got out. This egocentrism of his, a very peculiar one, as a matter
of fact, for it was often disinterested, sometimes trapped him.
I was a master at setting such traps; we worked together a dozen
years, after all.

Take the time we sat together in some center for the creative
arts near Warsaw, working on a film book or detailed scenario.
Suddenly Jerzy is called to the phone. It is the minister, summoning him for tomorrow. Later I overhear Jerzy negotiating
with the lady director about a seat on tomorrow's minibus to
Warsaw. I listen to this without batting an eyelid, for I know
the outcome.

About suppertime Jurek realizes that the minister is probably

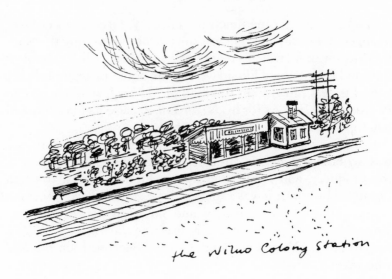

the Wilno Colony Station

not having him come to reward him but to have it out with him about something. So Jerzy says casually: "Listen, we have to hop to Warsaw tomorrow."

"We shme. You are the one who has to go . . ."

"Hey, that's a bit too easy! We are going together."

"We are not going together. I have no seat booked on the minibus."

"What are you talking about; I booked at noon, didn't I?"

"You booked for yourself, but not for me."

Jerzy shuts up, flummoxed. And he knows that I have arranged this predicament for him, as between friends. I hadn't breathed a syllable until it was too late.

Yes—Jerzy is an egocentric, all right. Yet in our film business, perhaps in my whole generation of filmmakers, I haven't known a more decent colleague. In this profession, which demands ruthlessness, egoism, and hard elbows, Jerzy really never failed me in all these years. By and large, he was loyal, conscientious, and scrupulously honest in all artistic matters. I said "by and large" because as an employer he sometimes exploited me; on the other hand, I was a pretty hardheaded and unyielding employee, and it wasn't easy to exploit me.

There is one thing, though, I am absolutely sure of. Kawalerowicz is the most film-wise person I have met in my life. He was, perhaps still is at times, an absolute phenomenon of directing talent. Somebody once said that Kawalerowicz has a film camera for a skull. And really, his is some uncanny sort of computer to which you feed a chapter of prose at one end and out pops a length of film with ideally directed scenes at the other.

Having worked with him so many years, I learned a great deal from him, both in the craft of writing, though he has not written a single line of his own in his life, and in the art of directing films. If some sequence found entry into his scene book it meant that there could not be a better one, that as a matter of course all possible variants had been worked out, tested, and rejected for one reason or another.

Hence Kawalerowicz's greatest strength and greatest weakness was, is, and will be the perfectionism that grows in him year after year, the overwhelming urge for the consummate achievement of the professional, of the craftsman of art in the way the Old Masters of the Venetian or Flemish schools were craftsmen.

Perfectionism is a dreadful daily affliction. It is a horrid monster that lurks in every line of the script, that paralyzes the flow of artistic consciousness to the brain. It is the terrible frost of the icehouse.

But I meant to talk about his exploiting me as my employer. We are working hard on a script, let us say, in his apartment, when he still lived near Union of Lublin Square. I smoke a lot of cigarettes; he smokes little, just randomly, when the whim takes him, not out of a fierce need like me. Eventually I run out of cigarettes. I ask if Jerzy has any in the house; it isn't worth the effort to go out to the kiosk. Without blinking an eye Jurek claims he hasn't any. I raise no question, although I suspect that he has, artfully hidden among his books, a carton of Gauloises, our favorite cigarettes. But when he goes out to the kitchen to see about tea I deftly extract a pack from the carton, unseal it with a flourish, and light one cigarette.

Jurek comes back from the kitchen. "Where did you get that cigarette? I thought you were out of them."

"I had forgotten about the pack in my jacket."

He eyes me suspiciously. "Here, I'll have one, too."
Magnanimously I let him have one of his cigarettes.
We go on working. I take a lot of puffs, inhale with gusto,
but he is gnawed by horrid suspicions. He helps himself from
the pack, he smokes, but without real pleasure. At last he breaks
down and declares, lost to all shame: "You took my pack of
Gauloises."

"But you don't have any, remember? You are always smoking
mine."

After a lengthy inner struggle, he finally laughs: "All right,
all right. I know you got at my carton."

Another time, unable to dig out from my entrepreneur some
monies he owed me, I requisitioned the dinner jacket he used
to take to film festivals. He had a new one tailored for him,
fashionably cut with rounded lapels, and I began to appear at
New Year's Eve parties in his costume. In those times dinner
jackets were a rarity, and my acquisition spurred a general longing. Someone was always borrowing it for a trip abroad, but
only I knew that the garment had a curse on it. Who knows
but that those three yards of cloth with their silken appurte-
nances had a spell cast on them by their former owner.

Be that as it may, I have never known another object that
has dumped a similar load of bad luck onto my acquaintances
and friends. Even Wajda reaped bad luck from this costume—
need I say more—although such a circumstance must seem im-
probable. Well, Wajda traveled in this dinner jacket, I think it
was to Venice with his film *Samson*, and returned without any
award. Even the Ecumenical one.

Jerzy Kawalerowicz has dropped out of my daily life, but we
do see each other from afar, we remember each other, we stand
by each other in rough times, may God ward them off. Long
live the good old Kadr, and we with it, alongside it, and far
from it.

One of Gucio's anecdotes: In a theater, during rehearsal, the
director insulted one of the actors, who submitted the matter
to the collegial court. The quasi-judicial body is in session, the
offended actor in attendance. The offending director appears

and addresses the plaintiff before the court as follows: "I wish to apologize to my colleague for this incident. I was excited, opening night is near, you know how it is. My temper ran away with me. It happens in every theater; take it as a sort of accident in the workplace."

The actor, in a tone of irritation, retorts: "Oh no! Excuse me! I don't think that's enough."

"Not enough?" recoils the director. "How would you like to kiss my ass, then?"

I don't know why this little tale came to my mind just now.

Ode to Liberty

All day I have been looking for some keys belonging to my wife, who is sojourning abroad, while the cat and I keep house in an empty apartment. Time was when two children disported themselves here, two daughters, that is, also my parents-in-law; whereas today the cat Ivan and I potter about, lonely as two thumbs and all unhappy. The cat because he is guilty of certain failings in the matter of personal hygiene and has been banned from Danka's room; I because I can't find the keys, a bunch of old iron in a leather case.

I even got quite worked up about it. My morbid imagination—which functions only in life, not in literature, more's the pity—conjures up a hundred variants of crime stories featuring burglary, or rather, effortless opening of the door, theft of the very manuscript in which I am at this moment drawing various signs and pothooks (writing a book, that is), the murder of a writer or, worse, the death of a celebrated cat from a heart attack.

I turned the house upside down. What I dreaded most was the possibility that I might have tossed the keys into the trash, as Dygat once did with a watch he had just wound up. So the trash can was subjected to a microscopic examination. But when near the end of that bright Sunday, a day for going out of town, taking to the water, dropping in on friends for supper, when near the end of that lost Sunday I decided to go down to the courtyard to the huge garbage containers to extend my search to that steel rolling stock, and first put on my robe, my elegant cherry-colored terry-cloth gown—to my jubilation and the cat Ivan's I found Danka's keys in its pocket. I had used them two days earlier when it turned out in the morning that the faucets were dry and I had to go to a street hydrant for water.

How many times have I not made fun of the absentmindedness and other little foibles of various colleagues! Now the Lord has punished me, and I forget everything and can't retain anything. After all, when I wrote *Anthropos-Specter-Beast* with reference to a film director who figures in that book, I portrayed a small part of Jurek Kawalerowicz. Among other things, I equipped him with a nervous tic, something like spitting with dry lips: as you would do if you wanted to get rid of a bit of lint stuck to the tip of your tongue.

Everybody enjoyed this very much, people who knew me got the point and snickered, and everything was fine. But one day, from early morning on, I began to do the dry-lip spit myself. Everybody noticed it and started to laugh even more heartily. But there came a point when no one felt like laughing anymore. I dry-spat from morning to night, at meals, at meetings, in church, on a rendezvous, in the cabinet minister's study, in my sleep, and even during an operation. My wife could not stand it anymore. The cat found it unbearable. When he crossed the room he kept ducking, as if dodging bullets. All the shooting, though, was done by me, from dry sore lips.

Later, however, turbulent events came to pass that we all remember, and I stopped expectorating and began to wait. I am still waiting.

The day is fading slowly. In the air, viscous with twilight, drifts the white down of poplar seed. Somewhere in one of the brick crates above or below me a child sings in a monotone, as I used to sing to myself in the meadows of my childhood. Today they pay money for such singing and such compositions.

Calmed by the recovery of the keys, I lie on the couch, which is fitted into my niche as on an airborne catafalque, for on this piece of furniture I undertake voyages to faraway continents and deep into space. I lie there thinking to myself and conclude, after many years, on the verge of old age, after all kinds of experiences, that freedom is the most important thing, after all.

There were moments when it seemed superfluous to me, a luxury, anything but indispensable. At other times I would forget about it altogether, or if I thought of it at all, I would engage in sophistic speculations relativizing the concept of liberty, grinding it down to a powder of equivocation or crushing it in a vise of ambivalence.

Yet now, at the evening of my life and the end of great upheavals through which it was my lot to live, it is my stubborn belief that this freedom is the most important thing, after all. I bear hunger with ease, stand pain tolerably well, but lack of liberty throws me into a state of heavy prostration, a sort of freedom-vitamin deficiency, a vehement craving for independence, a general inanition of the spiritual organism.

There was a time when they struck the word "freedom" from books of mine. I had had my *Anthropos-Specter-Beast* end with the words: "If we could only be well; if we could only be free." And that little joke, that travesty of a street saying, that concluding line of the book, was amputated by the censor. In my own country, in my own language, in my own book for children, I had to allow a nameless creature to cut out the little word for freedom, which all the world relishes at will.

And right now I somehow don't feel like trading merry banter with the censor serving on a future shift who will pore over my present opus. I don't feel like ogling and flirting when I refer to that value of human existence which once was ours in abundance and is now measured out in drams.

I have always been amazed, and am still amazed, by the people who consider that they have been accorded the right to limit other people's freedom. And that this right, this trumped-up privilege, this inhuman mandate was given them by Providence, history, or their own genius. And although they generally perish by the wrath of the enslaved, promptly successors turn up who get busy forging chains for their fellow men.

Freedom is spelled out on jail walls and over the gates of

prison camps. Freedom is found in the refrains of poems and on the tanned buns of nudists. Some are ready to throw up from a surfeit of it, others do not see a streak of its dawn from cradle to grave.

Are all of us now alive and in circulation headed for freedom or for the night of slavery? My dead friends, my brothers in hell or in heaven, tell me on some night crushed under the fearful edifice of a bad dream, or crumbled by stifling sleeplessness, tell me if it is worth it to fight to the finish for that winking cirrus of oxygen, that vanishing dot of rainbow colors we call freedom.

I look at this world in the bird's-eye view of some winged vertebrate that has fluttered into the frozen reaches of space and is peering from there at a bluish little planet that seems squeezed too hard by someone's fist, perhaps the Devil's, perhaps the Lord's. Why do those who bring freedom build prisons and organize a police force the next day? What makes victorious freedom fighters become gendarmes? Why does this thing called freedom have two faces like the moon? Why can we see only the shadow side of freedom?

The cat Ivan, my slave and master, has woken up. After some woolgathering in the easy chair he looks at me with enormous willow-green eyes. He knows everything, has secret, supernatural connections and ways of communication with other worlds, if such there are, with other dimensions of time and space, if God created such, and with the Spirit of Reason if It permitted itself to exist in a state of non-being inconceivable to us wretches.

I opened the door to the balcony for Ivan. Let him enjoy freedom. Perhaps he will later, or even now, intercede for me in the proper places. My days are numbered. But perhaps no one has counted them yet. From somewhere far away freedom is on its way to us. Its coming is an absolute certainty, although you can barely make out its loom in the snow, in gales, in rainstorms; in our dreadful disorders; in the whirlwind of our hysterias; in the ague of my death throes. My kind of freedom, which does not limit anyone else's.

But what will I get out of being free?

So Far and Yet So Near

I remember from childhood the watering of horses. By now this function has made it into the photograph albums and movie theaters. Film directors adore those little scenes featuring a sunset, water, and men on horseback. Naked men and naked horses. Archetypal rite and a heartthrob of romance.

In my time, though, this was a simple farm routine of broiling summers. You had to get washed up after a hard working day in dust and grit and swelter and give a breather to the toiling beasts, i.e., the horses.

People willy-nilly have always honored horses, although they are not especially bright creatures. For horses built civilization; it was equine muscle that erected that middling and not overly splendorous edifice of human civilization on a middling planet in the solar system.

But we did not give any thought in those days to constitutions or constellations. When the air cooled off drastically after a blazing day, and a twilight scented with gillyflower flooded the great gorge where the Wilenka flows, Uncle (Grandpa) Blinstrub and some kinsman and I rode our nags bareback to a place where there was a broad slope broken out of the high clay bank and the river made an abrupt turn to the south.

The air was cool, chill like a forest brook, but all else was deliciously warm, baked by our sun, that hardworking star, which made a job of it when it shone and when it heated a place. Warm were the horses' backs, the shoots of the bushes which entangled our legs and shoulders; warm was the clay of the landslide and the water of the river that ran so hurriedly toward the town.

First we bathed the horses in the well-known deep places of our river—more properly, our stream—which we called pits. The horses even did a little swimming there, dog-paddling in the dark water, which already reflected those brilliant stars of our sky. After that Grandpa (Uncle) Blinstrub hobbled their forefeet, and foot-cuffed by hempen gyves, they would hop-

and-shuffle clumsily on the dewy meadow; and the thumping of their hooves and their copious snorts accompanied our sober pastimes in the water.

First, though, we soaped ourselves on the slick clayey margin, narrow as a parapet, at the foot of the slope. Uncle Blinstrub lathered himself methodically and carefully from his head to his lean shoulders to his chest, which showed every rib, vertebra, and ossicle under the skin, down to the legs braided with hard muscles. I myself didn't touch the cake of soap with the stag embossed on it even twice. I swam all day from six in the morning; the moment they let me out of their sight, I plunged and dived in the greenish water full of spiny-finned miller's-thumbs.

The twilight deepened. Somewhere beyond the river at the edge of the great wildwoods, or perhaps in the forest itself, someone sang as if mourning some sudden loss, while we immersed ourselves in the warm black fluid, which might harbor some water dragons or drowned men; and I thrust with my legs against this water fraught with secrets, and the deep voice of it could be heard all the way to the Upper Colony.

But why do I recall all this? Who cares? Really, who cares? I do . . . Perhaps there is some cripple or mental case who does, too. Why should I worry about it ahead of time? "Who are you writing this for?" critics ask. "For readers," I suggest shyly. Surprised by my audacity, they come back with, "You probably write for yourself." I know what they have in mind. An ambitious author should write for himself. Finished. Period. But who I write for are the frail and vulnerable ones that knock about the world cracked, out of kilter, with teeth falling out and bowels out of order. I must have readers who are my equals, perhaps even a bit above me, who keep a watch on my hands, my eyes, my slightly skewed noggin.

Just a minute, I had a quotation ready somewhere. The following was written by a certain author a hundred fifty years ago: "It seems to me that ever since the world has been the world, there have never been such changes in everything as in the course of my life. For everything is different now: estate, customs, religion, people; so that, if a person whose memory does not reach back to our former times were to come face to face with what there was once, he would not recognize his own country—and even less would an old man brought back to life . . ."

I know that all old people have talked that way—in antiquity, in the Middle Ages . . . and now I, too, feel like looking behind me to see what size leap we have made in my lifetime, within my awareness, before my eyes.

Through my great-uncle and great-aunt I rubbed shoulders with the nineteenth century. I spent time in those hamlets in the Wilno country where no one had seen a train, a car, a light bulb. Imagine a little estate twenty miles from a railroad, surrounded by endless forests, thinly populated by Belorussians. And imagine an eighteen-year-old miss who agrees to a loveless marriage with a middle-aged clodhopper squire because her parents have so decided. And consider that this girl will live on this mangel-wurzel manor to the end of her life, and in the course of this life will meet illiterate peasants, now and then the parish priest at a church fair in a tiny township, and very rarely, once in a blue moon, some toil-worn, chuckleheaded neighbors. Nothing—no news, no letters, no music, no change, no hope. And picture the mail once bringing besides *The Polish Huntsman* a translation of a French novel by the title *Madame Bovary*. In those days, ladies and gentlemen, people *read*, literature had an influence on the reader; a book did not die on the vine in the hands of a jaded skimmer who kept a weather eye on a winking and babbling TV.

Yes, I spent time on such manors and granges. How beautiful this sentence sounds in a novel: ". . . but later he buried himself in his little rustic estate and, shunning his neighbors, lived his life out in seclusion." It makes easy reading, this sort of thing, and is good for a little romantic shudder, but just you try to put it into practice, try to use your own life to illustrate this lapidary phrase.

Yes, I witnessed time let loose and human life thinned to whey. I inspected the first radio, a detector, as it was called, which featured a silvery little crystal in a glass cylinder which you poked with a bit of copper wire, looking for the best re-

Danke with our tyrant

ception. Uncle Blinstrub with some cousin set up an antenna. He drove two poles into the ground like two masts, some fifteen or twenty yards apart. The tips of these tall poles were joined by the antenna wire, and when the installation was finished, I moved the wire on the crystal and heard in the earphones a far-off tinny sound of music.

Later at Aunt Pola's I saw a cathode-tube set. A hefty box sat on a stool, a glow and a hum came from it; Aunt Pola's husband turned a knob, and amid whistles and squeaks there would be a sudden fragment of human speech or the hurried sounds of a symphony orchestra.

I remember just before the war a children's magazine which invariably carried a column headed "Did you know that . . ." There was some discussion of experiments with television, meaning the transmission of pictures over a distance. But no great future was predicted for this invention. The trouble with it was waves that refused to bend. So I forgot about television for twenty years. It was easy to forget, for that matter, for life rushed along amid wars, occupations, and revolutions.

I was particularly impressed by an airplane, a silvery or whitish bird which used to cross our sky every day on a northerly course, headed for Latvia perhaps, or even farther. I said every day, but I suppose it flew once a week, and only in fair weather at that. I dreamed of this passenger plane a thousand times, and for some reason always saw it stranded on the sandy beach of the Wilia near the Bujwidze estate, lying on its side as though it had crashed. To me at this distance it looked exactly like a kayak with round headlights on its sides. In those dreams I ran toward this magic arrival from heavenly spheres, I ran as fast as I could but never once reached it.

I have given myself a break. For a week I haven't done any writing. In the afternoons I sat down to, or rather lay down to or hung over, the correcting of the typescript of my previous book. I howled with pain and despair; it felt like something written eighty years ago.

Total disaster. Attempt to induce death by the exercise of willpower. I was dying, dying, and couldn't bring it off. The first draft was a failure.

I had always known that I would outlive my books. But it's one thing to know it and quite another to savor that pleasure. My books, of which I never held a very lofty opinion, are beginning to die—quietly, without ado, on their own, without my consent, not gradually but at quite a clip. But why would anyone care? Umpteen thousand books, hundreds of films, millions of musical notes die every day. Who cares except over-ambitious authors?

Here I twaddle about how the world has changed in my lifetime. Was it to recede, was it to return to its beginnings? If it existed and lived, it thrust forward. In my childhood, atlases had white patches. This meant that on certain exotic continents there still remained unconquered and unexplored territories which the maps indicated by patches of white, i.e., blank areas of paper devoid of the slightest information.

In my childhood we used to collect the foil wrappers of chocolates in order to ransom a little blackamoor out of slavery. We weren't all that sure in what slavery these Moors lived, but we gladly collected the silvery wrappers. Now the blacks might well be getting their own back. In America I myself have seen solid black citizens being driven about in priceless Rolls-Royces.

In my childhood the moon was not yet a space port with rusting cans and wads of gum left by astronauts. Forty years ago the moon was the Moon. A mysterious, enigmatic, fabled guest from the cosmos, the finger of our Lord, and at the beck of this finger the oceans flooded and ebbed and poor humble man got out of bed at night and walked roofs and steeples with his eyes closed.

Also heaven, the sky. Who nowadays takes any notice of heaven and the other place, formerly full of angels and devils screening the sight of God? And what is it now? Now the vault of heaven is a superhighway traveled by astronauts and cosmonauts doing something or other, erecting, tinkering, and monkeying up something that'll be revealed to us in due course if we live that long.

Krzyżówka, the little manor of the Pieślaks, was twenty-some miles from us, i.e., from the Wilno Colony. When the Pieślaks set out on a visit to us, they traveled all through the night, in order to avoid the heat of day, and arrived at dawn. In winter, if the sleigh track was good, the trip was much faster. You bounded along to the tinkling of the harness bells, *janczary* or, as we called them after the Belorussian, *brazguny*, for just a few hours, perhaps three, perhaps four. Whereas nowadays our Warsaw playboys, when they have a bit of time to spare, get in their cars and buzz twenty, thirty miles out of town to paw a young lady in a fleeting extramarital "relationship" and posthaste return to town to work, for time's a-wastin'.

In my time, meaning the time when Konwicki was young and gay, a person who had been to America was a sensation. In Chałupy on the Hel Peninsula a fisherman was nicknamed "America" all his life because he had seen America. Today even I, who isn't always granted a passport (and I don't blame them), even I have been to America three times.

But what am I writing this for? Who cares how many hours it used to take some Pieślaks or other to get to Wilno, which is now called Vilnius? Who takes any interest in my childhood or the cat Ivan's? I have had it with my childhood, I have no more time for the Wilno country, which has sunk in the ocean of oblivion like Atlantis. What do I care about that Wilno country, which I used like a cane to lean on, like marijuana to dope myself with, like gilding to embellish, ineptly, an ill-favored life.

". . . I have thought to myself, not without a little malice," Antoni Słonimski once wrote, "that if the stage of Konwicki's youthful adventures had been Grójec or Sochaczew, he would have found it harder to charm us. Without the great avatar,* without the palladium of his word, what would that Tuchanowicze of his mean to us? Who would remember the name of the Wereszczaks' daughter?"

True—but even the avatar hasn't helped me much when all is said and done. Perhaps the thing to do is to take a hammer and smash the outdated pen once given me by Weber. But if I am not going to write, what am I going to do, how will I justify my existence? I have often dreamed of becoming a cloakroom attendant. I suffer from insomnia—what a delight it would be at one or two in the morning to hand out overcoats, furs, and umbrellas and collect folding money from tipsy suckers. But cloakrooms, I am told, are the preserve of responsible personnel of respectable services. A broken-down writer can't even get near them. Perhaps there was a chance once, when I was being knocked by *Trybuna Ludu*, while in the foreign papers my name was sometimes twisted to Korwicki, Kunicki, or even Kuropatkin, no less—the famous Russian general.

Christian Humility

With a nineteenth-century scientist's fervor I investigate the state of health of my environment (which is constantly undergoing changes and transformations within the social organism), the

* The allusion is to the foremost national poet of Poland, Adam Mickiewicz (1798–1855), who called Polish Lithuania his fatherland, and whose spirit still presides over contemporary literature rooted in the Wilno (Vilnius) region, like the writings of Czeslaw Milosz and Tadeusz Konwicki himself. [Trans.]

direction and intensity of the evolution my fellow countrymen are subject to. And among numerous scientific aids, specimens, fabrics, substances, there is also our press, i.e., the four Warsaw dailies—*Trybuna Ludu, Życie Warszawy, Rzeczpospolita*, and *Żołnierz Wolności*—which I buy every day at a certain stand and later read, collate, draw conclusions from with the utmost attention. It doesn't matter that these papers are practically indistinguishable. It may even be a good thing that the ordinary amateur does not see any differences among these products of the press. It is precisely this background of similarity that accentuates the power and significance of any differences. When we examine seemingly identical texts, we presently discover a great many telling divergences, nuances of formulation, the expressive force of emphasis. Even in a foreign newspaper I have found a photograph of my own humble figure wearing an outsize coat and a less than astute expression, but to make up for this, from the pocket of that coat proudly protruded a copy of *Żołnierz Wolności*.

So today, too, on a dull lethargic free Saturday, I root about in my beloved papers, worry a passage here, nibble at a couple of paragraphs of a news story there, touch a wary tongue tip to some ads; elsewhere immerse myself despondently in the obituaries, where for some time now they have persistently featured stiffs a year or two younger than I (and me still alive). But now all of a sudden my eye falls upon sections of an interview, quoted in the press survey column, with Jan Dobraczyński, the publicist and author of a great many books.

"I have a right to be content," Dobraczyński allows. "I have accomplished more than expected, it seems to me. I am read . . ."

The sycophant conducting the interview interpolates: "You are one of the most popular Polish writers. How many translations have you had? Hardly anyone has been, and still is, so widely translated . . ."

Dobraczyński: "There is still Lem! But I realize that I have made it. Unusual success. It would be difficult to quarrel with it. I consider that I have brought something off, the more so as I wasn't one hundred percent a writer."

"You weren't one hundred percent a writer?" wonders the quicksilvery sycophant and line feeder.

"Right. Those nothing-but writers, shut away in ivory towers painted all sorts of colors—'not excluding black,' as Iwaszkiewicz used to say—know little about life. Take me: I have been a civil servant, a soldier, a social activist, an organizer, a member of parliament, an editor—even a politician."

I promptly go all mushy over this, for it reminds me of my own high-wire act of self-advertising, the rule of my life and bequest to my descendants: If nobody appreciates me, I must at least appreciate myself.

The Will to Power

Sociologists, psychologists, men of learning are always holding forth about the terrible motor force of our instincts and drives. Dear Dr. Freud has so brainwashed us about the total fiendishness of our libido, a dreadful sort of *fatum eroticum*, all-powerful in this vale of, beg pardon, genitals, that we have allowed ourselves to be sidetracked, losing sight of the hordes of four-flushers, psychopaths, and wheeler-dealers who constantly, at every hour of the day or night, without surcease and with savage rapacity, elbow and scramble their uphill way to power, who want to dominate and subordinate us and stomp us into the ground.

The "sex drive," oh, my Lord, how comic and unconvincing it now sounds! It isn't so long ago that the professors saw a phallus *in statu erecto* at the origin of every event in mankind's history. With unheard-of tenacity they tracked down sexual complexes, erotic deviance, and frustrated love in every personage in the encyclopedia.

Yet now that all the taboos surrounding human sexual life have turned to dust, it is perfectly obvious what impels those hordes of people, what lends them superhuman strength and drives them into madness.

What it is is the will to power, the greatest energy immanent in our solar system, more powerful than nuclear energy. In the past, breeding, social discipline, and societal rules used to blunt or inhibit, perhaps simply hide, these drives in certain individuals. Formerly such a specimen, in love with himself and convinced that he had a God-given right to decide the destinies of others, was at least a little embarrassed by his aspirations, concealed them or gave them some protective shapes and colors; and these measures somewhat impeded his criminal instincts, attenuated them, or at least rendered them more bearable to us phlegmatic creatures devoid of ambition and enmeshed in scruples.

Today, shame is extinct. The market is clean out of it. One may find it after mole-like researches in forgotten archives hung with dusty cobwebs. The insolent power grabbers, if that isn't too clumsy a term, are rampant in cities and hamlets, in the echelons of government and in literary clubs, in conjugal beds and in cemetery chapels.

There is no point in expatiating on those unhappy lunatics who shoulder their way into politics in order to rule states, societies, or armies. We see them as clearly as the palms of our hands. Every day we nod to each other and tap our foreheads as we watch the TV news or scan the dailies.

But the subspecies of these that we have to put up with around us daily is another matter. For instance, I phone a colleague and say, "Let's go for a walk." He answers, "I can't." That's it, period. He can't—that is an objective, historical, irrevocable fact. But when *he* calls up and proposes a walk, and I say I can't, a severe interrogation begins: Why can't you, whom are you going to see, and what for? All of a sudden I become a defendant, a prisoner, a slave.

I dread social gatherings like the plague. Formerly it used to happen that one did a little talking and then politely listened to the other person. Now everybody only wants to hold forth, dominate, impress. People gather in living rooms around dubious potions and unwholesome dishes and gab, prate, blabber, gush, preen, boast, show off, swagger, pontificate, levitate. No one listens to anyone. All keep their mouths in rapid motion, emitting through those evil maws torrents of lightly compressed air.

Unable to cope with this pestilence ravaging contemporary

humanity, in my humble way I try to weaken its aggressive force somewhat, deflect it into a black hole or abyss. For the know-it-alls, for instance (who also illustrate the urge to dominate, of course), I prepare purposeful traps. I make up a twisted form of some foreign expression, get a historical date wrong, or give a moderately distorted summary of someone's book. This gives me half an hour's respite while the unleashed know-it-all corrects me, instructs me, supplements my education, preens his feathers, soars above me by levitation, and from his height releases on me the droppings of his knowledge, competence, and superiority.

All my acquaintances and non-acquaintances want me to see the movies and read the books they do, go to bed with the young ladies they have fancied, worship the leader they adore.

For here it needs to be noted (this is my own scientific discovery) that those thirsting for power and dominance over others may at a completely unexpected moment experience a sudden fascination with someone else's power and, as though by an act of biological or biopsychic expiation, to make up deficits, as it were, in the cosmic energy balance, fall on their knees before someone else, put his foot on their neck, and become his slaves forever.

There is a crazy, hysterical movement going on in this sphere of human activity. Now they are on your back without respite, and you run out of strength to throw them off; a bit later they kowtow to someone else like puppies, like young animals manifesting their submission and dependence—as Konrad Lorenz has observed—by proffering their tender rear ends.

Both I and my daughter Marysia have this instinct to dominate, manage, and what goes with these, to possess, but with us it is on the wane. This is why both I and my Marysia almost automatically assume the part of bystanders, accompanists, admiring spectators. We listen attentively, nod our heads, choke up with admiration, surrender to aggression (provided it doesn't interfere with us), bear with the whims of power (when they happen to suit us). And everybody loves us, craves our company, praises us to other bully types.

Marysia and I have our hands full. We could make a fortune out of this casual catering to our power-hungry fellow men. But to make money out of the frailties of others isn't fair. That's why we serve acquaintances and friends scrupulously and disinterestedly and put in a certain amount of effort—but only for a time. Suddenly we get bored and depart, leaving the client in black despair.

There is still another domain. It is somewhat shocking, and I enter its territory with some embarrassment. I am thinking of the swaying of souls, the sport so beloved in Polish art. That competition is entered in this country by all who have some sort of facility with the pen, the brush, or the film camera. To rule the souls of contemporaries; carry them away; turn them into angels.

About this sway over souls—a concept probably unknown to other nations—an unending, merciless, bloody struggle is waged. They don't begrudge you a fortune or success with the ladies, but they won't forgive you a dominion over the moody souls of their countrymen—the idea that you might take a place next to Mickiewicz and Wyspiański and reign over the mysterious, capricious, magical spirit of the Poles. That's the real thing.

The idea is to be admired, worshipped, honored, and kick one's neighbors in the teeth, elbow them into a black pit of abasements, drown them in the silent river of nullity.

It is a curious thing that I chose "Christian Humility" for the title of the previous section.

Shelved

I acted in a movie today. Just like that. They sent a car for me, I got in like a matinee idol and was taken to the set. There I waited long quarter hours in a room offstage for the crew to struggle with the lighting and the camera, which had jammed and wouldn't stir.

Usually I was the one who was bustling all over the set between lights and camera while the actors watched me expectantly, craning out of dressing rooms, minibuses, bushes. But today I was the actor and saw this entire shooting day from the other perspective, a very dull and exhausting one.

I watched somebody take my place for the cameramen, whom our confidential jargon calls crankies. I listened as the sound lady discreetly conferred with the director on the problem of my unfortunate voice, which resembles the croaking of an old prostitute soliciting a sozzled client.

In the end everything worked: I came together and went into gear. I projected ease, sincerity, a direct relation to life; I also did my best *not* to project, suddenly to be myself, sparkle with intelligence, glisten with nuggets of thought, and get a laugh by nonchalance; and when it came off, just as abruptly move them with a touch of real emotion. In a word, I acted my head off in a film that was predestined to become a storekeeper, meaning the kind that from the instant shooting starts everybody knows is headed for indefinite storage.

This is because the film will be a film about myself, i.e., an unpopular person who really shouldn't have a movie made of him; nevertheless, or perhaps for that reason, one is made anyway, so when it is done it will go into cold storage along with other miscarriages.

Clearly I let myself in for a pretty ambiguous undertaking; but I do it, after all, because the picture, or rather film essay, is directed by Andrzej Titkow, an intriguing poet and gifted director, whom I have known for years and whom I like and respect for a special kind of principled and incorruptible artistic integrity.

While I am on Titkow, I can't resist the urge to mention the way a newspaper covered a documentary film festival at Oberhausen a few years ago. If I remember the report correctly, it said that some of the awards went to the Polish directors Titkov, Andreyev, and Shulkin (names as Polish as Tolstoy and Rasputin), others to Russians: Zamoyski, Kowalski, and Nowak (names as Russian as Paderewski and Piłsudski) . . .

All day today, as I acted and perhaps hammed it up a little, the thought of that last book that didn't come off nagged me like a toothache, not to mention the redundant one I am now writing or the future one I have outlined for myself but am losing faith in, and which will probably come to repose on my own private shelf, never even begun.

Shelf. Personal shelf, city shelf, government shelf. I have the feeling that in the course of this summer, which has suddenly turned icy cold and rainy, I have been clambering of my own free will onto a shelf—the huge broad shelf where you find so many writers and so many works abandoned or stillborn, aborted by the authors' own artistic organisms or by government obstetricians.

Another case. In my neighborhood, a few streets over, virtually next door, a fellow artist whom I have always particularly liked is dying. Actually, he is no longer dying, his struggle must already be over. But the machinery of medicine, that proud achievement of our time, still tosses his poor carcass about, simulates life by inflating him with oxygen, whose aroma he no longer smells, and infusing him with blood which refuses to struggle up the conduits of his arteries to his lifeless heart.

This is why, alone in the house with the cat Ivan, forsaken by wife and children, I have climbed up to my niche (perhaps it is all right by now to write *nitch?*) and am trembling with cold, or is it despondency, my own particular shakes, which sometimes die down in me and then unexpectedly get worse again and worse—but who cares to hear about someone else's jitters?

Ivan is no help. He is preoccupied with his old age. After Danka's departure he began to, I don't know, grow senile at a rapid rate, lose his marbles, turn into an old fogey. His fur is still full and beautiful, maintained by me with the aid of various feline vitamins and pills. But that mug of his, that inane snout with the slack of his tongue sticking out! I am simply embarrassed to have strangers see him. I flick that idiotic tongue flap with a finger, but it doesn't help much. I hold a mirror up to him so he can see for himself what a cretin he looks; he pretends not to see anything. Cats always ignore mirrors, and I bet it means something. They know what is good for them.

I wish I could reach for the trusty bottle as I used to, down a quick couple of shots, and, slightly numbed, plunge into the darkness of a dreamless sleep. But these days I dread the shot glass like the Devil, I cross myself over and over at the sight of a decanter, so I guess I'll merely turn from side to side on the shelf where cruel life has deposited me, give a low moan, sigh, and lie there meekly until morning comes, the early dawn of summer, thank God. Good night.

Sick

I woke up at intervals throughout the night. I felt flushed, hot as on the beach. I pushed down the bedclothes and stuck a leg out from under the blanket to cool it. I was thirsty, so I went to the kitchen and drank vast quantities of water out of a kettle that smelled of old boilerplate. Then I began to be afraid. I was seized by the sudden panic associated with an abrupt loss of breath. I lacked the air and the strength to go on living.

I dragged myself from the couch, trotted in a tight circle in the middle of the room, and returned back to my niche. If I "returned," of course it was "back." But adding "back" accentuates this return, dramatizes the situation, adds a touch of malignity to my predicament. I returned, then, to my niche, which blazed like an oven, and as I did I saw that Ivan's eyes were open just a tiny slit. He was lying on his side in the armchair and gazing at me without compassion and with a bare minimum of interest in my movements and operations at such an unusual hour.

I, too, lay down on my right side. The right side is my good side. On it I go to sleep and spend the major portion of the night. The left is only used once in a blue moon: when the right has a broken rib or is strained from the endless toil of hefting my corporation, which is often heavy, but at times becomes lighter when I am engaged in slimming down.

Toward morning I felt in my throat something like a fishbone or a tiny burr or a whorl of nylon thread. I spent the rest of the night trying to force that foreign body down my cankered throat and not succeeding. Then I reached for the fever thermometer, but it somehow slipped through my fingers and broke into smithereens. Droplets of mercury jumped all over the floor, and Ivan observed this ballet of quicksilver beads in silence but did not stir from his place to chase the unknown little creatures; for some time now the cat Ivan has not hunted anything or anybody. Impudent flies buzz past his eyes; sometimes one will land on his nose, but he doesn't move a muscle, just follows the pesky insect with his eyes as if he were a guardsman appointed to his post by the cat god.

I began to rummage in the cabinet where we store outdated medicines that no one needs. I found another thermometer, sitting in a glass tube for tablets because the cardboard box where it belonged had some pipette in it. I stuck the instrument under my arm and looked quizzically at those Polish, Soviet, French, or German medicines. Should I throw them away right now? Get rid once and for all of this garbage that clutters up the cramped apartment? Yet perhaps tomorrow or the day after they might come in handy, might be needed, and no pharmacy will have them in stock. Every few days I use eyedrops bought in a pharmacy after expiration of the legal storage period. I squirt in a few drops and wait until evening to see if they help, or further irritate, my bloodshot vampire eyes. (Artur Maria Swinarski once told Krzyś Toeplitz, who was a powerful, dark-haired man, "I love those eyes of yours, Krzyś: black and red!")

How can I be in any mood to throw away medicines when my temperature is 37 Celsius? To me, to my organism, 37 is a high fever. Danka has 39 at the slightest provocation; she goes to bed and sleeps through twenty-four hours like a good girl. I have only once in my life had even 37.5. It takes a lousy 37 degrees to make me go into delirium and pass out. Thirty-seven degrees. My heart pounds like a pile driver ramming posts into the sea bottom. Paroxysms of wild panic. Run out into the street, rush among people, plunge into life. What people? What life?

I lie down on the disheveled couch, which looks as if it had hosted a difficult birth. It is still a long way to go till morning. Morning, my own breakfast time, when the cat Ivan and I proceed to the kitchen.

The view from the window is the kind poets love. Blushing dawn, the first stabs of sunlight, an early-morning breeze casually ruffling the poplars that have grown up around the parking lot practically as I watched. But I don't want to see any of it. I am drowning in night sweats and cruel horrors. Getting sick in the middle of summer! Those chronic daily ailments that keep accumulating are not enough: in order to coddle, defer to, wait on this ever more demanding system of mine, I have to devote an hour and a half to it every morning. It's an ordeal; it drives you up the wall.

Sick and lonely in the middle of summer, a real summery summer (here I may be overstating it a little). O wicked fate, O baleful destiny! Yet there had been such a promising horoscope this year for Cancer, that is, for the suckers born under this sign. And if the earth's population is almost five billion now, those born under Cancer make up about 400 million. Four hundred million people are waiting three-hundred-odd days for a lucky break, an unusual opportunity, a geyser of happiness. How could Providence possibly make four hundred million people happy? When there is an overall shortage of happiness in the universe, anyway?

Awful fever, awful sweats, feeling awful . . . The thing now is merely to survive until hospital opening time. Hospitals never close, of course, what I mean is the arrival at the laryngology clinic of my dear, beloved professor, who has poked, cut, or stitched in my throat quite a few times. Consider, though, that just last night during the soccer game between France and Yugoslavia they showed someone dying at the Yugoslav bench. Some coach or team physician, perhaps, instantly lay down flat, and before you knew it, he was doing mouth-to-mouth, people were massaging the man's thorax, bringing up a box with dangling cables. Over there on the field they kick each other's ankles, fling each other to the ground, dash back and forth like crazy, and one wonders what it all means: for over there by the sideline a man dies before the eyes of fifty thousand people, while here a rite takes its course which nothing must interrupt. Even if the earth were to split and gape open, play must go on and goals be made. The whole world looks on. The whole world has paid its money. The whole world is our master.

The players see out of the corners of their eyes that their leader is dying. But the opponents press on and want to kick a goal. Stand to attention and salute, or kneel down and say a prayer, or announce a time-out and a minute of silence? Such moments of hesitation, perplexity, indecision are born and perish in this arena where twenty-two men in club colors and three in black sweep back and forth. In addition, three dignified roosters bestride the grass, very conscious of their importance. The French fans have launched these live symbols of Gaul in order to dope their players into heightened aggression. And indeed, the Frenchmen in undershorts swarm all over the field, although by the sideline a totally obscure Yugoslav is expiring, a Serb perhaps or a Croat or Slovene, or even a Montenegrin. The TV cameramen discreetly pan to the motionless form on the grass and someone's hand rhythmically kneading that figure like the plastic lid of an empty box.

At this point something drops on me, some black weight plumps onto my sore rib cage. It's that fiend, the cat Ivan, who could not care less about my afflictions, my terrors, my literary tragedies, which I cannot confide to anyone in my quest for sympathy and surcease. The dumb old brute has jumped on me because he has been waiting all night for me to wake up. He likes to jump on my chest without warning, knead it with barbed paws, crawl in circles in search of a suitable spot, and suddenly flop down into my warmth and break into a stentorian purr that can be heard by passing pedestrians.

This cat, which was to be my daughter's property but became my proprietor, is indifferent to my minor and major crises. But is there anyone who isn't, actually? If I ever do complain to somebody, the upshot is always: "Don't dramatize, you are always pouring it on so thick." When I start on my death agony, my friends will smile good-naturedly: "Tadzio is kidding again."

If one could just reach the stage when one can go to the hospital without embarrassment or fuss. Go to the hospital and find out that everything is all right; that all it is is a slight laryngitis, that I should gargle and drink that chalky mess, that I have a long sandy road yet before me, featuring a lot of rain, wind, snow, heat, a long unnecessary way, leading nowhere. Lord, have mercy upon me if I sin.

A State Park

I open the Polish-language newspaper published in Wilno, the well-known—to me especially—*Red Banner*, and am pleasantly excited to read the following:

PAWILNIS STATE PARK TO COME INTO BEING
This decision will contribute greatly to the preservation of the natural features of the landscape of eastern Vilnius and its topographical and cultural relics, which represent scientific, aesthetic, and recreational assets. The area of the park will comprise 4,500 acres and include the picturesque districts of Pawilnis, Leoniszkes, Barsukine, Rokantiszkes, Sapiezyny, Puczkoriai, Lyglankiai, Belmont, Markucziai, and Rybiszki. For the protection and proper utilization of the green spaces a special forestry district is to be created. A detailed utilization and development plan is being elaborated, and appropriate regulations will be formulated. The planners envisage an area-wide recreational development of the natural resources available, such as the basin of the Wilenka and the hill and forest areas. Thought is also being given to the adaptation of the terrain for skiing, sledding, bicycling, etc. The productive utilization and management of the park will involve a number of ministries and agencies. Overall responsibility has been entrusted to the Executive Committee of the City Council of People's Deputies of Wilno.

Ah yes, of course, dearies . . . "Pawilnis" means the Wilno Colony, "Rokantiszkes" is Rekanciszki, "Markucziai" Markucie, Belmont is Belmont, and "Puczkoriai" must be the ancient, mysterious, magical Puszkarnia. Polish place-names remaining in Polish phonology, and Lithuanian names once Polonized and lately Lithuanianized again. All of the Wilenka valley from Nowa Wilejka to Wilno. Five miles of a prodigy of nature which took shape over millions of years, the eighth or perhaps eleventh wonder of the world, formed by the action of floods, earthquakes, and glaciers in order to provide the setting, in due course, for the advent of little Tadzio Konwicki, prophet of the people, proletarian bard, Lithuanian magus, and magical Pole.

a certain acquaintance from Wilno

The Wilno Colony, Upper and Lower, the universe of my youth, my own personal cosmos, whose thraldom I did not leave and never will—a state park . . . In a commonwealth which contains Lake Baikal and the Pamirs, the Amur Basin and the Kola Peninsula, the Kara-Kum Desert and the Black Sea coast with the peaks of the Caucasus. The Wilenka, our swimming hole in summer and skating rink in winter, where we caught fish and pneumonia, the innocent little stream we used to drink from and, at times, beg pardon, pee into—that Wilenka of ours was now a national park in an empire that stretched from the center of Europe all the way to the shores of Japan.

My heart is hammering. It pounds like the Old World sledge-hammer my father used to wield (if he wielded one). After all, I myself played a small part in the mythologizing of the Wilenka valley, having contributed to that amazing exaltation of a pro-vincial watercourse in a minor canyon lush with vegetation. My enduring worship, of forty years' standing, of this dot on the map of Europe, my persistent weaving of legends around a countryside quickly forgotten by everyone, my tenacious loyalty to a minor fiction that occurred to me once in my life—in short, those almost invisible efforts of mine, couched in bad Polish, those unlettered wails and broken sighs finally compelled a deaf and blind fate to place the Wilno Colony (or—I should spell it correctly—Pavilnys) among such global entities as the Egyptian pyramids, Niagara Falls, the Côte d'Azur, the Grand Canyon, Venice, and St. Peter's Basilica in Rome.

I quickly lie down on the couch, or I just might burst with pride. The cat Ivan has a belly ache; the poor brute storms about the apartment emitting tigerish snarls. National park . . . Our Lady of Ostra Brama! And here people wonder where I get those astonishing talents.

But my love for that valley is disinterested. I return to it only in my thoughts, in sudden pangs of longing and in fever dreams. I don't ever want to go back there as a revanchist. That gorge and the city at its mouth is the old capital of the Lithuanians, our brethren in sins and holiness, with whom we created that Commonwealth and with whom we laid it into the grave.

A national park—an odd spot in the middle of Europe, but a little to one side, as it were. Mine, yours, ours held in common.

A Subversive Prank

I went to see Lusia, my cousin, whom I have known since she was a child—I even have a dim memory of her coming into the family. More than that, I remember her parents, still Olek and Wacia at the time, going through the internship of engagement then obligatory, and even before that, the immensely complicated rituals of courtship. And these days Lusia, herself, already widowed, has taken up "bioenergetic" therapy, and I am one of her patients and have the impression that those musicohypnotic sessions actually yield a degree of relief from the multifarious complaints that loiter indecisively about my system, unable to take a definite direction, hither, thither, or yon. The doctors are already up in arms against the motley quackery of faith healers, swamis-from-the-mysterious-East, medicinal herbs, springs, and muds, all those radio-esthesias, bioenergies, psychotronics, what have you; even the minister of health has shaken his finger at those hyphenated hypesters. Yet from time to time I drop in on Lusia, just in case. How many things have I not done in my life "just in case"? Perhaps I even live just in case.

However—originally I meant to say something else; namely: this is the second time in a row that an Olympiad will be held in a reduced condition, boycotted by various groups of states. All my noble colleagues and also the more sentimental armchair fans, all those tradition-minded and not overly bright types shed tears, wring their hands, even tear their hair if they have some to do it to. A great calamity, a moral disaster of mankind, the destruction of what was virtually a religious rite of sport and soul.

As for myself, though, I rub my hands with glee. I take pleasure in this sudden and unheralded demise of contemporary sport. Let me remark timidly that as early as the Munich Games, when the Israeli athletes were murdered in the Olympic Village, I wrote, I called out, I shouted from the housetops that sport was sick. But nobody cared to hear. Too many people have a good thing going with sport of whatever variety. Sports are an enormous industry, a gigantic entertainment multinational, a world bank that turns over billions.

Athletic competition has been taken over by the state. In a number of countries, it is a government operation like the police, the army, or the mining monopoly. It is countries that compete in the stadiums, states that go to war in the sports arenas. To many countries, professionals are their live torpedoes, the range of athletics their neutron weaponry.

All breakthroughs of science, the finest research in military, cosmic, and genocidal medicine, the entire technological effort of midget statelets and superpowers alike they invest in sports— so as to see a garish sheet of linen or silk hoisted as high as possible, and to hear those monotonous phrases of pompous music called national anthems played as often as possible.

Look at the ever-swelling hosts of invalids, freaks, and hybrids: they are the athletes of today. Our heroes. The brothers of the ancient Greeks and Romans. Anabolics, steroids, blood transfusions. Doping and forced training. Regimentation and galley slavery. Fraud and abuses.

Sport as we now see it has degenerated, gone insane, turned into a monstrous thing, something like an epidemic, a general agony in an aura of crime and sin. Contemporary athletics is dying and should be allowed to die as quickly as possible. Let every vestige of this bizarre and appalling deformity disappear.

Then, years later, let it begin a humble new existence in villages, hamlets, remote settlements. Let ordinary boys and normal girls, as we once knew them from books, pictures, and our own youthful dates, secret rendezvous, bashful puppy loves—let those young people begin again to play ball games, do gymnastics, swim for pleasure's sake, for fun, to kill that specter time that hounds us on every hand as long as we live and, for all we know, beyond the grave.

Let lean young men and comely maidens take up sport for its own sake again, let them get joy and amusement out of it and gain strength for work and gaiety of spirit to overcome evil in this world. Let them run, and jump high and long, until once again someone takes money for a jump, another takes steroids to make her run faster; until once again shameless predatory governments lay their greedy paws upon those harmless provincial stadiums, and once again it will become the most important thing in the world *whose* colors will be hoisted higher on a white stick and whose anthem will be played oftener on this chuckleheaded globe.

Mushroom Hunting

The literature of fact. I am the fact of my literature. Treatment: Lithuania. Literature of fact. Very well, then.

I was walking or, better, trudging, shambling, slogging through the wet forest, dense with silvery cobwebs outlined in droplets of water, glittering nets hung between tree trunks, among dripping bushes, and on huge motionless fern fronds. Chilly drops kept falling into my collar, on my forehead, on my hands, which were already furrowed like washboards, as I surveyed pillows of green moss, dun mounds of dead needles, thin stacks of dry oak leaves. What I was doing in these woods between Augustów and Suwałki was looking for mushrooms. But the mushrooms weren't many hereabouts; I was wandering through these wildwoods laid waste by the ravages of man, war, and time because there I always seem to hear the organ drone of the Wilenka as it speeds toward Wilno, to pick out among the forest sounds the pealing bells of bygone years, and to feel overhead the cold air from Dźwina, Święciany, and Santoka.

Suddenly I look up and see a female sitting on a stump. She is wearing the trousers they call "britches," but untied at the ankles in the sort of Soviet style now much in fashion. Over these she has a flowery skirt, that too quite modish. Her prominent, somewhat outsized head is ringed by an aureole of bristling matted hair *à la* hatchling chick. Her map is painted, especially along the cheekbones, a little like the makeup of TV announcers; the upper works are stuffed tightly into some sort of military tunic from the last war, German possibly, or British.

This babe, not old yet and potentially quite good-looking if she was to throw fashion to the winds and wash up a little, this babe smiles at me, I can't tell if flirtatiously or knowingly, and here in the middle of the wildwoods that stretch all the way to Latvia, Belorussia, perhaps even Mordvinia, this babe with the equivocal little leer addresses me, unasked, as follows:

"I know, my poor buttercup, that you are wandering through these woods with one thing going round and round in your head: where did it all come from—this life, this being of ours, this . . . existence. The foreign term we use in order to make the idea sound more serious. Am I not right, sweetie pie, you wrestle with higher problems? You don't care about our everyday things—unused meat coupons, kids with worms, a stupid bill in the Sejm. You are seeking God, in order to grapple with Him, wrestle Him, pin Him to the mat, as you tried to do some little classmate in a meadow on the Wilenka."

She fell silent and awaited her effect with that sly leer which, I decided, was lubricious, after all.

"And you know everything, I take it, you old witch," I said, licking droplets of forest water from my lips. "Someone told you in the wee hours in Warsaw as you were reading fortunes from grubby cards by a hotel wall. Probably some Arab, perhaps a Filipino, most likely a tourist from the Easter Islands. So tell me, if you know so much, and then I'll answer."

The fortune-teller (or perhaps not that, just a summer female in a flashy getup) started to puff a waterlogged spider—which had been sliding down a spruce branch by its thread—off her nose. "You are looking for a sign. For almost sixty years you have been on the lookout for a secret gleam to light everything up. And I have waylaid you here. Lured you out of the capital and then stepped in your path in this forest, where a dead man lies under every tree. Not just dead, but killed by another man."

A breeze brushed over the mountain, scattering drops as big as gooseberries all around.

"And so?" I prodded the witch.

"We are biological robots in revolt."

"Oh, come on, what next?" I remonstrated.

"Oh yes—someone has already blathered on this subject. Someone has perhaps already had a hunch about that pedigree of ours, which is technological, not in the least divine. But what I said about this revolt was really just for myself, to cheer myself up. We aren't in rebellion, all that has happened is a new consciousness, not foreseen by the engineers, our creators. Consciousness is a divine attribute. That is why they deported us— meaning you—to a vacant little planet, without major prospects, in a tiny planetary system sentenced to perish within a short span, less than a billion years, and dissolve into nothingness. You yourselves have inscribed that derivation of yours into your collective memory: the awakening consciousness of self, the expulsion from the primeval homeland, the yearning for the engineers who summoned you out of non-being, and the prophecy of a return to the place that exiled you."

"And you?" I asked the enchantress, or rather, perhaps, the lecturer in cybernetics.

"I am an image. A reflection of some form of existence, some thought, some unfulfilled promise. I myself am not, never have been, and never will be."

"But come, don't I know you from shady little dinners, from wild debauches at night, from petty orgies among office workers? You swilled home brew and necked with various sheiks and lounge lizards between stacks of coats in entryways. You drag yourself through life, don't you, constantly changing your plumage, driven by some female urge or perhaps by despair. Dried-up crone or neutered codger, little pile of biological junk, pinch of phosphorus called by some cosmic cataclysm to exist in nonexistence!"

"You all have been put away in a dark closet, like a useless broken piece of equipment, and forgotten. Your sufferings are senseless, and your sins won't be counted by anyone."

"But who are the engineers who produced us?"

"People."

"How, people? *We* are people, after all. You, I, that someone who is calling in the middle of the forest by the lake. Those are people."

"Yes, perhaps there are people among you. Strayed there by mistake like grains found in chaff. But I don't exist. I rebounded from the depth of the lake or the forest wall and am already ricocheting back into the darkness, which isn't darkness. For that there is darkness and light, life and death, good and evil, is only an illusion of yours."

"And who am I? A person turned robot, or a robot turned human?"

"You'll find out before long."

"Stay!"

"I can't."

"Wait—I am about to remember something."

"You won't remember it. It's too late. You have already almost forgotten it altogether."

"The country here is the vestige of an umbilical cord."

"The country here is the vestige of . . . the country here . . . the country . . ."

I was walking along, or rather trudging, shambling, slogging through the wet forest, dense with silvery cobwebs outlined in droplets of water, a forest between times gone by and the present, which escapes from underfoot and flies, flies with a dreadful roar like a cataract of stars into an eternal darkness that is not eternal and not darkness.

Literature of fact. I am the fact of my literature.

Farewell to Wilno

If any time in my future life I am caught mentioning the Wilno Colony, the Wilno country, or Lithuania once more, let the nearest passerby shoot me without mercy. And if he doesn't happen to have a gun with him, let him strangle me. And if he doesn't have hands (one time, before the war, Father Rękas, patron of the sick, began a radio chat by saying, "I've received a letter from a woman without hands or feet"), let him poison me.

I can't break away from that Wilno, from that hybrid land that is both Lithuania and Belorussia and neither; I can't unhook, unglue, tear loose any more than that Oszmianian or Mejszagolian insect could in the sweltering years of old, from its flypaper, which smelled of honey, foaming-fresh milk, and bruised blackberries. But whoa! I am off again in that direction, starting, on the spurious plea of authenticity, to recall those years, which are long forgotten and of no concern to anyone.

Actually, no—the fact is that right about now, out of the blue, Lithuanian Poles or Polish Lithuanians are turning up again. I have just finished reading, have put down only this morning, as it happens, on a dull Saturday morning, a book by Jarosław Marek Rymkiewicz. I mean Jarek Rymkiewicz's book *Polish Conversations, Summer 1983*. I am slowly collecting my thoughts, a little daunted but also cheered, astonished and uplifted, disheartened and full of zest . . . for what, that's the question.

Just a while ago I described mushroom gathering in the Suwałki country; why there, exactly, I don't know myself, and why in the presence of an almost house-trained sorceress who nevertheless hailed from Lithuanian heathendom. Now here in Jarek's or Marek's book, Jarek-Marek has mushroom hunting, too, and in the woodlands of the Wijuna River, sacred snakes, witches of Poland and London, devils pro- and anti-government.

Some sort of sorcery is at work here, some charms operate at this season of shortest nights and longest days. But I know what is behind it all: Jarek got a doctorate in Polish philology, he wrote fine books full of scholarship, he was a poet from the university and wrote beautiful academic verse. But something abruptly rebelled in him, kicked against the pricks, howled like a wolf, and Jarek-Marek suddenly found himself jaybird-naked, like a draftee at inspection, confronted by Wilno, Lithuania, Belorussia, ambushed by memory or the vehemence of quickening imagination.

I don't know what the facts are. I am not about to investigate his genes, aunts, or birth certificates. He is a true Lithu-Pole by force of voice, temperament, imagination. Out of his narrow, learned, professorial throat a deep bellow rumbled forth like an old bison's, muscles started rippling on his powerful bull's neck, and he snorted fire and brimstone from his black nares.

I salute a new fellow countryman, I incline my silvery temple before a younger Lithuanian and allot to him the whole county of Oszmiana from Dźwina clear to Siemiatycze. As for me, it is time to wrench the rest of my paws free from this bird lime ashimmer with every rainbow color in an awesome, murderous blend that rivets you to an authentic and invented past, to something that once was but by now is careening across the ninth galaxy from ours in the allegedly infinite universe.

Farewell, Wilno (how many times does that make?), welcome, vast new city stretching from the Bug River to Gibraltar, or even from the Urals clear to the sequoias of San Francisco Bay; welcome, megapolis, in whose far-flung sections you may suddenly hear a timid singsong accent and an incomprehensible word—you guess Sanskrit or Hebrew; you may catch a stealthy cursing or blessing gesture that minutely changes the course of the world, the rotation that is ever slower and more ponderous,

marked by the squealing and groaning of an axis long unlubri-
cated at its polar bearings by the Lord.

But before I say goodbye—assuming I ever do say goodbye—
in other words, before something irrevocable happens, before
I make a fateful decision, right now, at this moment, before the
sun goes down (though it is setting already, has set, dragging a
veil of red after it into the stellar abyss) I still have to tell about
a meeting, a strange tête-à-tête meeting yesterday, of the shock
it was to me, and perhaps to him, too.

I was walking along Krakowskie Przedmieście, not far from
New World Avenue, the avenue I have written so many pages
about and plan to draw illustrations of in due course; not far
from New World Avenue, then, but closer as yet to Palace
Square, in the neighborhood of the corner house of Miodowa
Street, or Honey Lane (must all cities have a Miodowa Street?),
at the foot of that house, more properly at the black sluice that
comes down between the slabs of the sidewalk; by the black
sluice, then, and why there? Because there was a faucet there,
not a hydrant but a simple tap, evidently a prewar one even,
for it was a brass casting. So it was by this faucet that he squatted,

I knew him at once, in squashed moccasins of sorts, God knows whose hand-me-downs, some street Arab's probably; he squatted by the wall, the projecting base of it, actually, and collected water into a little aluminum mug, though in fact the water ran from the faucet into the cracks between the slabs of the sidewalk, and what he was pouring into his mess can was a viscous yellow liquid from a flask, which immediately put me in mind of olive oil, good Greek olive oil to dress a salad of lettuce with or perhaps a dish of chopped vegetables or fruit—and I realized he must have carried or shipped this habit, or rather this favorite dish, or more exactly its recipe, with him from the shores of the Bosporus,* and so he was preparing this little exotic dish for himself—and I stood there like a plaster statue, goggling with eyes that were beginning to burn and chafe in their bearings, I mean the lining of the lids.

It was he. There couldn't be any doubt. He wore a wide-brimmed brown leather hat, a trifle cowboy style, but it could just as well have been worn by the Spirit of the Steppes or some outlandish cavalryman, or a palmer from an unknown land or colony or dominion or, most likely, protectorate. Never mind about his hat, though, which took me aback, seeming a bit out of place and suggesting some sad derangement in its owner. More important under the circumstances (for identification, of course) was his face: tanned, with a slightly olive tinge, at odds with the aesthetic criteria of Nowogródek; never mind, though, either, about the flesh tones of the old man's face (not all that old, actually, no one would credit him with those nearly two hundred years): the most important thing was the growth of hair on it, that amalgam of beard and sideburns, the thick fringe running from his ears under his chin like some displaced half-halo of pepper-and-salt whiskers—pepper-and-salt, *nota bene*, not yet altogether white, though they ought to have been all white, or even green or purple after overcoming the first silvering that hangs on five to ten years—that beard, nevertheless, that flat bolster of thick hair on which his strong prominent

* Adam Mickiewicz (see footnote on page 157) was a native of Nowogródek and died in Constantinople. [Trans.]

chin always rested, that thatch of his we all know and remember from old engravings or illustrations in books and reference works, and that gaze of his that could have been romantic, disdainful, surprised, or vacant.

So he was squatting by the tap, clearly getting ready for lunch; this was the proper time, too, around four, when we used to have it down in Lithuania; and Lithuania meant a whale of a spread of country, after all, all the way from Volhynia to Kurland. He was evidently preparing his meal, and doing it with such ceremony that even a soda-water peddler at his carbonating cart raised his eyebrows and stood gaping at the aged seer in the faded Old Polish tailcoat, casting spells over a tiny mug in midsummer, 1984, blessing the food perhaps or singing a Belorussian chanty remembered from childhood—as it was sung on the banks of the Switeź two hundred years ago.

I hadn't the slightest doubt that it was he. He had finally chanced to Warsaw. For the first time in his life. He had been on the road a hundred fifty years, roaming all the countries of Europe and veering into other continents, for all we know (hence that somewhat feebleminded hat, we may conjecture). There had been a rumor—deliberately launched by somebody, perhaps even himself—that he had died of the plague. It was a fashionable death at the time, you could hide behind it. I have known many who did in my time. I shan't mention names, for no one has authorized me to. I remember particularly a certain composer of the seventeenth century. His ocarina dated back to that era, too. That is why nobody talks about this; why there is a conspiracy of silence.

At this point the clock in the spire of the Royal Palace with all due ceremony began to strike the fourth hour. Ordinary four o'clock, or 1600 hours, not twelve noon or twelve midnight; not even six in the morning or nine in the evening. Just the humdrum knocking-off hour of Polish office folk. But it was Sunday anyway, so there weren't any civil servants about. But he raised his exalted face upward, skyward, and began to improvise. Obviously no one observed this creative act, this burst of inspiration. And I recognized only by the movement of his livid old man's lips the individual words that were so close and familiar, pronounced with that peculiar accent, that character-istic intonation. Like my mother's, surely like my father's, whose voice I had never heard; or could not recall if I had.

This was a short improvisation. I am sure of that, because for some time I have been familiar with improvisations. There comes a season in our lives (if we are from down there, I mean), a moment when suddenly, out of the blue, we begin to improvise. I have had that happen to me when I was alone. Like an epileptic seizure. There was no one around to notice, luckily.

He was improvising. His eyes turned back in their sockets. But that face, I swear, was an old man's, yet ageless. No one would have taken him for more than a hundred, hundred twenty years old. And it came to me all of a sudden that for some higher reasons, divine counsels or the Fiend's design, he had been hiding among men for two centuries and might yet roam a whole millennium in this terrible farrago of guilt, misery, torment, and chaos, reciting verses to himself at odd moments, in those microquavers of time, and that I would trail him down the ages, and when our path would ascend, I would see those who went before him, and looking back, I would see those trailing behind me. For he who has once spoken the Word will forever exude the Word like blood in an unending hemorrhage.

It is night, but not deep night at all. Night is at its onset, just starting. But I am quaking in my niche, shivering again and convulsing. I know. I see it clearly, understand it as keenly as can be. All have gradually lost their minds. Individuals first, then clusters of people, eventually entire strata of society, and finally nations. They all went insane before my eyes. Lunatics govern, lunatics pilot planes, lunatics sell cereals in the shops.

Alone among lunatics, I am normal. A single solitary sound mind amid deranged patients, inmates of a vast insane asylum from pole to pole, from ocean to ocean. What am I doing here among madmen as alien to me as stones, mountains, clouds? Alien and mute. Alien and disturbed in the head. Whom have I to commune with, whose breast to sob on, whom to ask for absolution?

Alone among madmen. The most terrifying kind of loneliness.

Incident

Twice in my life have I been struck in the face or, in popular terms, poked in the snoot. The first time was in the dim past, long before the war, in the legendary days of childhood. I was in elementary school, eight or nine years old. During the long recess a lot of us, smaller and bigger ones, were gathered in the middle of the gym. We weren't fighting or scuffling, it was merely that something interesting was being discussed. And out of the blue, for no reason whatever—that's how I felt, at any rate—a junior-high strongman aged sixteen or so walked up to me and struck me in the face. And then, as in some dumb tale, he gave a long laugh, one of triumphant insolence.

Greatly hurt by this incident, I resolved to wait until I was bigger and our powers would be more even. But the moment of tasting revenge never arrived for me; early in the war the athlete—whose name escapes me—was killed by a train.

The second time I got it in the mug was at the verge of old age, on a January night in 1968, from a Polish militiaman. He was able to perform this with some emphasis and considerable swagger inasmuch as I was in handcuffs. The funny thing was that one of the three militiamen, who was in a prankish mood and intrigued by the occurrence, had a number on his sleeve which reminded me of the date of one of our historical uprisings. Most likely it was that of 1863.

But that time I was not thirsting for revenge. I could have lodged a complaint, brought charges, battled for justice. I came to wonder, though, why I shouldn't take it in the kisser, that it would establish something that the next man could not easily disparage, something that I probably had coming to me for a whole long life.

I take comfort from a kindly fantasy in which this former

militiaman, surely a pensioner by now, on one of those long winter evenings when the flames blaze brightly in the fireplace tells his grandson about the time he pushed in the jaw of one of them dodos as writes books they larn you in school.

I placed the above little episode in my *Calendar and the Hourglass*—at the time. Of particular interest is the passage about the militiamen. What sarcasm, and at the end, that cheap shot! Insolence pure and simple. When I read that lighthearted bit of persiflage over today, I shake with shame and anger. Fortunately, a judicious censorship cut that passage out, so the book was not disfigured by it.

A few dozen lines of text, yet how many distortions, falsehoods, and half-truths! It is true that I was detained by militiamen at night, but in what circumstances, on what sort of occasion? Let us bring out the facts: Of a winter night I reeled out of a certain dance hall stiff as a log. Well now, was the sight of me to be allowed to contribute to the corruption of such children as might chance to be out on the street at night? Come now, was I to be left to shock nuns of the night or foreigners gone astray? Quite enough falsehood and obloquy is trotted out about us in the foreign press. Little wonder, then, that the police took an interest in me. They drove up in a patrol car. One of them got out and asked for my papers. When they read my ID out loud to each other, I began to groan and grumble and mutter into my beard instead of maintaining a quiet and respectful attitude (for policemen are working stiffs, too, after all, only with nightsticks).

This being the case, the militiamen invited me into the car, and there, in order to forestall any damage to its costly equipment that might be caused by an inebriated individual, they made use of manual movement restraints (formerly "handcuffs"). I, brought to the level of the beasts by the intoxicant imbibed, began to maunder something to the effect that being handcuffed had never happened to me even during the Nazi occupation. Quite apart from the impropriety of this gibberish, my condition pointed to a partial loss of consciousness at the very least. In view of this, one of the functionaries, doubtless trained in medical first aid, initiated efforts to bring me to—resuscitation, as it is called. He proceeded as every physician would have: he stimulated circulation by vigorously slapping my cheeks with his open right hand, thus gradually restoring consciousness.

Because it was feared I might not be able to return home unaided (remember that it was midwinter, and the militiamen had reason to suspect that I was homeless, as is the case with some people), they transported me to a drying-out center.

There, unfortunately, they were received by an arrogant young doctor, who after superficial inspection—he never even troubled to take my temperature—after a very cursory examination, I repeat, pronounced himself unable to admit me to his establishment. The officers, men of experience, spent some time trying to convince him of the necessity of retaining me in the center, where I would receive proper care, a bath, appropriate pharmaceutical remedies, and a neat clean bed in which to sleep off my condition. But that impudent pup with his medical diploma turned on his heel and stalked off.

The frustrated officers, rather than abandon me in snow and ice, gave way to a humane impulse and took me to the precinct on Wilcza Street, where they accommodated me in a comfortable warm little room bare of any objects I might injure myself with in my state of intoxication. Before that, they had painstakingly recorded my personal data, lest I got lost in the paper maze, for that, too, is apt to happen.

In the morning I was taken to a nice, cultured officer, before whom, unfortunately, I began to raise complaints, my system having clearly failed to rid itself overnight of the alcohol consumed at the dance hall. He politely heard out my nonsensical charges, then said jocularly: "On your way . . ." But perhaps that wasn't the phrase he used, it may have been a humorous "Scram!" or "Out!" I can't be sure myself after all these years. But what I do remember well is that I caused people doing their duty a lot of trouble, irritation, and unpleasantness. And on top of that, I later made a point of describing them in a way that would serve as my revenge for the benefactions I had received.

And then, the business about the officer's number. What of it that this was 1863, conjuring up the date of the February Uprising? Any four-digit number may be associated with some historical year. What if this officer had had the number 966, the date Poland received Christianity? Or if his sleeve had borne the number 1410, the year of the battle of Grunwald or Tannenberg? So what?

Variations

I repeat myself. For thirty years I have been repeating myself with an indomitable tenacity. I repeat myself in my plot structures and in the positioning of my protagonists or, more properly speaking, of my constantly recurring protagonist. I repeat myself in the matter of landscape and setting, season, incident. I repeat myself in my psychologizing tendency and my jocular tone, in the paper and ink I use, in my orthographic and stylistic errors, in failures and disabilities.

But actually, why do I repeat myself? After all, the Lord has created me capable of fabulating and of effective narration instinct with charm and humor. I could have taken the place vacated by Miss Rodziewicz or, with some exertion, seized the scepter of Makuszyński. Prose, light but sincere and occasionally moistened by a little tear, is precisely what I am made for. I would have no difficulty presenting, in fluent, well-turned periods, the most unheard-of things, the kind that appeal to the reader, any reader, including the yahoo and the Zoilus of the bar counter.

So why do I repeat myself? Why do I keep grinding out the same grist of things that were and never were, things intuited and invented, felt to the full or never experienced? Why do I forever tread water and overuse the pronoun I? Why do I bore or infuriate readers and our glum and owlish critics, assuming they have made it into the present?

I *enjoy* repeating myself. I have a propensity, a morbid yearn-

the Cat Ivan submits to Marysia's affections

ing for repetition. Repetition is what bulges in my head instead of brains, what pulsates in my veins. I have hardly reached for my pen when I am seized by revulsion against any of the varieties of noble prose created by Our Lord, and want nothing so much as to repeat myself, continuously and endlessly.

The multiplicity of repetitiousness. The circularity of it, the involution, the echoing rhythms, the wheels within wheels: a spiral fastened at one end to the black wall of the universe.

In order to kill the gland that causes the anomaly of repetitiousness I would have to kill myself. That gland sits in the right hemisphere of my brain. I feel it bulge and dig into my skull with a spiky foot. But perhaps it has lodged in the lungs that once, between the Nalibocka Wilderness and Cracow, became impregnated with the resin smell of our woods and the fragrance of anemones and the bouquet made up of glowing peat, the alien frowst of exhaust gases, city sewers entrusted to this day with the remains of men murdered decades ago, and the reek of an ingesting and excreting city which is still alive today but may be extinct tomorrow.

I have heeded all the injunctions of the Russian philosopher

Bakhtin. The precepts he laid down for literature in his time in the Gulag I follow, religiously and strenuously. Like a lab animal I undergo torments to provide practical proof of his premises. Why do I conform with the canon of some maniac of literary theory, although I could have chosen not to? Why do I obey him although I haven't read a line of his works or ever held a book of his in my hands?

Repetition. Multiplicity. Circularity. Spirality. Cerebral palpitation. Cardiac microexplosions. Ascending rhythm. Until the black wall bursts.

I had come into a church. But even this sanctuary was full of lunatics. Very pious lunatics. Some even stepped up to take Communion. Does Our Lord use a special language to communicate with lunatics?

But I get more and more normal. The world is going mad, and I alone continue in mental and spiritual health. People go out of their minds, so do animals, rocks. What is awaiting me among the madmen? Perhaps I had better pretend to be mad, too. Perhaps the majority of these lunatics *pretend* to be loony.

I live in a reality that is cobweb-thin. Behind me and before me there is vacancy, the void, nothingness. I live in a reality that is as thin as our earth's atmosphere.

And what about a sense of humor?

The two saddest months of the year may well be July and August. You are alone at home and alone in town. Everybody has gone away somewhere, driven by some atavism, biological, astronomical, cultic. The longest days of the year, the shortest nights. Nature unbridled, licentious; mad riot of shapes and colors; apogee of life; explosion of vitality; all-embracing resurrection.

And I am on the sidelines, not participating. All by myself with the cat Ivan, a cross-grained beast that tyrannizes and bugs me, constantly wanting something, bored, splenetic, always underfoot, demanding to be entertained; abruptly he will tear about the apartment like a bat out of hell, then crawl on me, wanting to lie nose to nose with me, subordinate me to himself, annex me, annihilate me.

The summer is billowing, wallowing on top of me. I look at it the way an old pike peers across a pane of ice at approaching spring. I don't suntan, I don't run along beaches, don't bathe in a river or lake. I wait out the summer. Autumn is on the way, my personal new-year season.

When did this happen? When did I drop out, opt out, stop taking account of summer? All my life I had loved summer, greedily pecking up every grain of it. I was the one with the deepest tan, the one who swam out farthest from the shore, the one most strongly infected with midsummer-night-fever frenzy. I pursued life and clung to it as it rolled tirelessly along like a rustic wagon on a sandy road in August.

Everybody had left town. Danka wasn't here—but she was always away in the summertime. No friends or colleagues were around. A lot of them had left for summer vacations from which they would never return.

What does that sun shine late into the night for? Why do those little birds like chimney swifts flit like mad over the hot, slowly cooling roofs of the city? Why does a stray whiff of night-scented stock contend under my balcony with the stench of motorcars? And me alone. Perhaps forever. Perhaps this is my last vacation, from which there is no return.

I remember the first love of my life. I remember now, and will always remember, the moment when my heart gave a lurch like a combustion engine and began to rumble and rattle.

My first love was called Wisia, plain and simple Wisia, for she had been christened Jadwiga, and at that time all the girls saddled with such patriotic or historical names by unfeeling parents scrambled desperately for decent abbreviations; which is why the place swarmed with Jagusias, Wisias, Gogas, and Jagódkas.

For my first love, then, I drew one of those dreadful Jadwigas. But nothing could disfigure her. She had thick hair the color of rye, plaited into a braid or else two pigtails; she had a blooming, lightly sun-touched complexion, the kind they used to call peaches-and-cream, and lovely lips. She was standing in the road before me, an ill-favored classmate squirming next to her, for in those days out of mind, every pretty girl had to have an ugly sidekick. She stood before me, bouncing off her knee a black satchel (which she had let me carry from school for her earlier), stood before me in the full sun, against a background of blue sky full of white cloud piles, smiling a little, not without a touch of coquetry, a flirtatious glint—aware as she was, the minx, that I was eager to gain her favor.

Mother of God, how sweet it was to be standing in the road like that, looking at each other, and to make a date to do our homework together.

This was half a century ago. I was eight or nine. I never met her again later, and I don't even know if she survived all those idiotic wars, mass migrations, vast social shock waves. But perhaps she did come through it all and lived to know a mindless old age, white hair, and repulsive dissolute grandsons who dye their topknots blue or red.

I consist of particles, chemical chains, genetic ciphers which formerly circulated in the great tumult of my world and the universe we share. I am made up of clouds, trees, flowers, and proud cats.

And later, perhaps quite soon, I shall again dissolve, scatter, be distributed over my world and the universe we share. Once more I shall live, endure, exist in the rain, in rock, in a passing bird.

Also in a bundle of waves which, swift as thought, will dart along the black walls of the universe among water lilies of galaxies, running, running—where to?

Never again will I use the punctuation we always called the "question mark." Never again will I set a query between my rickety sentences. I don't need one anymore.

I am looking into Stanisław Cat-Mackiewicz, whom I love, and loved back then, when he was living and sometimes lurched heavily into the Writers' Society café, dragging behind him a beautiful and forbidding load of the past: sins, folly, insularity; at the same time, of a splendid courtly charm, exquisite intelligence, understanding open to anything. I looked at him with alacrity, anything but handsome though he was, after all, looked with some pride at our coming from the same corner of Europe, the same countryside, even, possibly, the same tangled pedigree. And to this day I like to read him, with unvarying fervor, although he has been dead for almost twenty years. Others have wilted and faded into a melancholy grayness, but him, stalwart bison with his great noggin full of impractical wisdom and very practical prejudices, him I still read with the same relish he used to show when reaching for the Russian writers of the nineteenth century, whom he ought to have detested but whom he loved with the tenderest filial affection. So in opening one of the books of this unsuccessful Lithuanian politician and magnificent, fortuitous, quasi-unintentional writer, I open a little old book, yellowed and printed in an outdated orthography, and read, suddenly enraptured:

So in those years—we speak of Piłsudski's youth, i.e., of the years 1867–1890, as well as of the later period up to the outbreak of the Great War in 1914—we observe in the Lithuanian gentry a strange tendency, not upward but downward, toward renunciation and descent down the social ladder. This was manifest in dozens of families, and the mood of the time, that "spirit of the age," was sympathetic to this renunciation and blessed it. In the squirarchy and gentry of the Congress Kingdom, the rump Poland created in 1815, the horse collars in Cracow glittered with black lacquer and silver, well-scrubbed britzkas and cabriolets shone gleaming yellow, the vehicles bobbed along on English springs, their coachmen's livery buttons sparkled, sportsmen gave away guns at shooting parties. Up in Lithuania, barely a handful of families gave themselves over to a pretentious style of life, trying to glitter, impress, fascinate after the fashion of the Kingdom or Galicia. On the contrary, a large percentage of the gentry simply went downhill: the old pier glasses in the parlors became clouded with mildew, the old vehicles were shut away in the coachhouses to rust, the hounds gnawed their flea bites on ancient, never renovated settees, flies in busy black swarms covered the food on the tables, grass overgrew the paths in the parks and pleasances, family papers were used to put under pound cakes and Easter loaves, and passionately, from dawn to dusk, the aristocracy was denounced and ridiculed, almost as if it were the "class enemy." I must point out that these phenomena occurred in very old and very authentic noble families, and that the elements in that class who dressed up and strove for a show of elegance and refinement could the more easily be suspected of descent from jumped-up estate agents and the *nouveaux riches* who had made their piles only in the early nineteenth century; a thing that by the peculiar notions of democracy held by our landed gentry was considered singularly repulsive. There was something very odd about this; one wonders if exhaustion following the Uprising had something to do with it, or a disinclination for energetic efforts toward domestic reconstruction ("organic work," as the slogan of the time called it)? Or was it the general mind-set against economic rationalism and resource development, which indeed did characterize very strongly the environment in which Piłsudski grew up? Or the disdain of St. Petersburg, careerism, money, and the corresponding idealization of poverty, abnegation, and sacrifice? I am the last person to glorify or go into raptures over this collective mood, which smacks of secondhand Tolstoyanism; I brand it as a mark of abdication and voluntary fall from status, I consider that it was precisely here that there resided those anti-European mental attributes which Count Sforza derides and which I discussed in the preceding chapter. And yet, recalling those irrevocably bygone times today, I must confess that to me there was a certain grandeur in this. Civilization consists in the creation of wants—and here were people who instead destroyed the wants they still had in childhood. But overarching it all was a kind of idealism; at any rate, it did not flow from sloth or passivity, it was something that was in harmony with the collective conscience of the era, with democratic stands, with contempt for money. For that matter, who knows what quirks and crotchets hid under the cobwebs of those sunken times.

I can't uncouple myself from the Wilno Colony. That tiny summer community, that miniature quarter on the periphery of Wilno constantly surrounds me, beleaguers me, hems me in. Hardly have I laundered it away, wiped it off my weathered memory, when it will treacherously float up from remote continents, perhaps even from another world. It will drift overhead in a rainstorm, on the morning star, but also by ordinary jet plane.

The day before yesterday I was lying in bed with a sleepy Ivan on my belly and, as usual before going to sleep, settling accounts with my conscience. Actually, what I am after is my life's annual balance, for my private year's end is approaching.

So I am dozing there, brushed by bad thoughts and ill forebodings as by bat wings, when all of a sudden the phone rings. My phone has been ringing seldom lately, and when it does it means a wrong number or some awful bore who has something unfit for human consumption to bring me, the kind that makes one want to hang oneself on the spot.

The phone rings, as I say, and I lift a languid receiver and murmur hello. I hear an unfamiliar, slightly foreign-sounding voice, stammering and groping awkwardly for forgotten nouns and adjectives. But presently the voice gets on the rails, as it were, finds the nearly obliterated track of memory, and is on its way—my way—with a stream of flawless Polish. And I learn that my interlocutor is Abba Kovner, an Israeli writer come to Warsaw in order to confer the medal of the "Righteous Among the Nations" on the former prioress of the convent at the Wilno Colony.

I am slightly stunned; I croak something into the receiver, I give a dazed moo or two, for where is Israel and where is the Colony, how does the little convent connect up with those trees planted in the name of "the Righteous," what has my humble self to do with any almost divine sublimities?

"Why, I remember that little convent," I say. "I've written about it in my books. I can see before my eyes the sunny forest slope between the Lower and Upper Colony and that timber lodge, or was it two lodges, with some sketchy sheds and barns built before the war on a mound like a vast petrified ant heap."

"I've just done some reading in your books, you see. That's why I'm phoning."

me in Dzieringin on the Narew

"That's the place where Wilner was in hiding during the war. I only found out about this recently from Hanna Krall's book on Edelman."

"I hid out there myself. Many Jews found refuge there."

"How many? I remember that knoll rising from the trees and the nuns digging seedbeds and weeding them. All of the Lower Colony gazed at that convent like at a star traveling low over the horizon, signaling the Angelus by the thin tinkle of the Ave bell."

"There was a time when we outnumbered the nuns. And afterward we returned to the ghetto and took up the fight, and later we organized the Jewish partisan units."

"Yes—I've been to Rudnicka Wilderness, and I saw your abandoned bunkers there."

"I read about that, too, in your book. Come tomorrow to the ceremony for Anna Borkowska, the prioress at that time, whom we used to call *Ima*, 'Mother'—from the Hebrew."

Next morning I met a *pretty* old lady, dry as a stick, with a face full of wisdom and nobility. And I met Abba Kovner, who spent forty years searching for nuns from the Wilno region who were scattered all over the world; searched with a quaint persistence, and in the end found this prioress and another nun near Cracow; caught them on the brink of the grave in order to hand them this most beautiful award ever devised by man.

In a little hall, in humble surroundings, sustained in body and soul by Józek Hen, I dissolved in tears, racked by emotional shock and trying to control spasms of sobs; a little swollen, too, with patriotic pride in the hamlet I had steadily extolled in the face of your disbelief; enormously honored that I, too, had some share in this little tree of "the Righteous," that at least one minute twig, ever so parched perhaps, belonged to me, too, because, sinner that I am, praying every day at the call of the Ave bell, I lifted mine eyes every day to the wooded hillside that rose above us like the rim of heaven.

I felt the fearful punch in the rib cage of a powerful attacking predator and, awaking instantly, looked into the grinning mask of the cat Ivan, who, his costly fur beautifully washed and groomed, stood on top of me and looked into my eyes with urgent expectancy.

It goes without saying that I realized at once what was afoot.

"Absolutely, Ivan," I said. "On this your birthday, as you complete fifteen years of life, permit me to express to you my warmest wishes for many happy returns, good health, and every possible success."

To wish him success like that came the more easily to me, since his good fortune, of course, is linked to mine. The cat accepted my felicitations most graciously, breaking into a powerful purr and rubbing against my brow, my beard, my knee under the blanket, also the wall, the cabinet by my couch, and the telephone, which latter evinced faint signs of life without, however, further response.

The cat jumped off me and led the way to the kitchen and the icebox. For all my strenuous efforts, I was still without meat. So there was only cream (a whole saucerful, regardless of gastric consequences), then a beaten egg; and finally, under the nagging stare of the celebrant, I proceeded to boil a young broad bean. This is one of Ivan's greatest delicacies—if the time is right, that is, for my cat is capricious; I know, because I have borne his whims for fifteen years. Everybody has vacations, everybody is free to come home drunk in the small hours, everybody is at large and unfettered; only I, alone in the whole world, languish in shackles, as they used to say. Indentured to a feeble-minded cat, I have no future.

Through all of yesterday I haven't used a single vulgar epithet with reference to this cat, although I stock thousands of them in my mind—owing to my origin in a place where two great universes of curses, insults, and blasphemous abuse intersect. All through the day I spoke to Ivan in hushed and softened accents, chose my words with care, and more than once drew on edifying maxims in the West European languages I know.

In the evening I had to go to a play, so Ania and her husband, Jacek, spelled me in keeping the birthday child company. They also brought some repulsive beef ribs with scraps of meat on them, which later in the night I scraped free of unspeakables, scalded, and presented to the celebrant, who had meanwhile entered upon his sixteenth year of life, his sixteenth revolution, sixteenth round of the solar system in the company of the hapless Konwickis.

I must just briefly mention the play, which was not eclipsed, after all, by the cat Ivan's festivities. For what I had managed to catch was the premiere of Wyspiański's *The Wedding* in Dejmek's production at the Polish Theater. And I must say a word about this, because for the first time in many months of theater a whiff of greatness wafted from the stage.

When the curtain rose and the audience saw before it a peasant hut—but enlarged and transfigured somehow, with implements and trappings magnified in proportion, as if we were looking at it all through a magnifying glass—and when the actors suddenly entered this vastly expanded reality, the spectators gave it an ovation, for they realized that they were going to witness an event that would make theater history.

I don't know what the wiseacres will say, but I was powerfully impressed by this shrewd and willful spectacle, without one note of music, without obtrusive blood-and-soil-mongering or that repulsive phony folklore stuff our imbecile directors have accustomed us to. What I saw was simply a European performance of a European drama, not some species of holy-roller play over which the natives dissolve in tears while on normal people, the ordinary *Homo sapiens*, it acts like a Chinese sermon.

Then there was my beloved Gucieńko, who has established his overall dominion over the magic world of theater, who by his mere appearance on stage induces a strange *frisson* in the spectator, or simply galvanizes him by his inner electricity: Gucieńko was at once given an extraordinary personal ovation, of course, and could have left for a card game with friends; he didn't, though, but showed up at the end among the actors acknowledging the applause. Another actor it was a pleasure to watch was one I claim for my own: Andrzej Łapicki, whom in private we call Łapa. Andrzej's treatment of the Poet differed from what he had done with it in the past. He created a less blatant character, free from accents of scorn and, instead, full of lyricism, meditation, discreet nobility. It was a joy to behold.

I am writing this with precious Waterman ink and am determined to engrave that evening in my memory, like that sunset, magic time of day, that gave me the rare chance to pass beyond the horizon of the common into another dimension of thought and emotion.

Later, toward morning, a terrifying tempest broke. Thunderclaps struck one after the other; the earth was drenched by a tremendous rainstorm, or rather, an entire great cloud filled with water burst over the sleeping city.

I woke up and saw every lightning flash even through closed lids. I was visited by an indolent thought: One should describe this early-morning tempest, insert its miniature portrait among all the other items of one's life, immortalize it as a thing of poetry and grandeur—as all the leading literary lights do, all the high priests of art domestic and foreign who magnify and emphasize to heroic proportions their transient spell on this strange sky-blue pebble that has been flying for billions of years through a black void. Or perhaps it is stuck in one place, arrested by the hand of a wrathful Lord.

From my childhood (in a place I won't mention because I am tired of it) I remember our dogs, Alsatians, all looking alike, and I remember them in unceasing motion sweeping across the space between the house and a feed bin or manger, in eternal bondage. Each wore a collar with a sturdy metal ring hooked to a heavy chain, the last link of which slid along a stout cable stretched between the house and the feed bin—really just a shed holding farm implements. This is how all dogs lived in those days, in a yoke of shining chain and on a steel line which allotted them a modest path of life, a short track for adventure, a tight arena for victories and defeats.

And I, too, wear a magic chain around my neck, which to you looks like a Dior tie or the collar of a shirt by Yves St. Laurent, and I, too, run only so far in my life as I am allowed by the invisible cable stretched along a shallow canyon—properly speaking, the trench called New World Avenue.

Perhaps this little blister of the universe's explosion is jocularly called New World by the gods of other, more splendorous universes. No interrogative here. Down with question marks!

Eschatological syndrome? Congeries of eschatological complexes? It's simply an illness. A disease of idlers and derelicts. Not so long ago my new world was still covered by two miles of ice. The north bank of the Vistula near Czerwińsk was the lip of this glacier, which has now retreated who knows whither. The scholars say that there is no God. This means that everything is God. My learned friends—they fry fish caught in the river, drink wine imported from France, worry about bad relationships at the university, and disbelieve in God.

From Ilya Ehrenburg's memoirs I recall again the sigh of some Soviet teacher: "There is no God—but there *is* cheese?"

* * *

A dreadful suspicion has haunted me for some time. Could it be that the people who sic us onto neighbors infected by greed for material riches, driven by a (not really terribly pernicious) instinct of possession, ownership, even egoism—that these rascals (I suggest this diffidently) seek to hide from us in this way their own pernicious greed for power, their fearful instinct to rule over their neighbors, their appalling urge to dominate? They steal our peace, our honor, and our liberties, roaring "Stop, thief!" at the top of their lungs.

Way back, thirty-seven years ago, I embarked on my worldly life. For hours I lay in a tight little room and looked through the window at a patch of sky. From this fragment of blue and clouds I tried to gauge the weather. There were heat waves, rains drumming on the sheet-metal parapet, showers of hail, doleful sleets, dusks and evenings, while I lay there, lay and lay, waiting for life.

And now, today, I lie in a similar box of brick—my niche, which has barely room for a couch and a small cabinet—and look through the window at an ample segment of sky, much larger than years ago; the sky has expanded, or I have moved closer to it. I look at this strip of blue, which in a while will change to the dark blue of clouds filled with water, or to the tousled column of smoke that always issues from the hotel. I gaze at this sky of mine for hours on end, with the cat Ivan on my stomach, my chest, my feet; endlessly I gaze, not waiting for anything.

Is it a good thing not to wait for anything? Perhaps it is lighter, easier, more pleasant. Yes—it's dandy not to wait for anything.

I am told that someone waits for death as if for a sure change of fate, a stimulating event, one more of life's adventures.

Variations on my theme. My variants of myself. My own vast variation, which gradually quiets down in me, and when it dies down completely, I, too, will have grown mute forever. Come to think of it, though, all the waves I have stirred with my laughter, my groans of pain, cries of delight (have I ever cried out in delight?), all these vibrations must have wandered on somewhere. Perhaps they are beating against the walls of this universe of ours like flies in a jar.

Everybody writes. At this moment thousands of people, white, black, yellow, good and bad, fortunate and down-at-heel, yes, at this moment thousands of people, perhaps many more, yes, certainly many more all over the world are writing at this instant that they are writing, as I am writing that I am writing.

The Southern Cross

I am traveling, endlessly traveling by a people-mover that looks like a gigantic rubber doormat. The pace is slow, and it seems to me that if I had stepped off the belt and walked, I would have got there long ago. But everybody is traveling by this conveyor along a corridor a quarter of a mile long, all the whites, blacks, yellows, and in-betweens. Some clutch the handles of suitcases, others the hands of sleepy children. A window shows a dirty December dawn that might hang on for many hours; I don't know if what we are seeing is full daylight by now or still the matutinal convulsions of this awful time of year.

Right now I see behind the panes a gray, ragged mist, parts of buildings showing through chinks in the mist, portions of enormous transcontinental airliners awaiting their turns.

My stomach has tightened, risen, imploded, and is now the size of a hazelnut. I feel it beneath my sternum or between my ribs, very much inside somewhere, where it aches, sucks, pulsates. The fact is, I am in a funk in the face of this scary and possibly unnecessary trip.

I am riding down an immense passage in the Frankfurt airport, looking for Gate 44, from which I am going to board a jumbo jet of the Australian Qantas airline. I am gliding along a mobile walkway constructed by the clever Germans, and am scared to death. I am an anti-traveler, anti-globetrotter, anti-pilgrim. What do I need all this sort of thing for? Why didn't I find the courage to decline those kindly, if somewhat stilted, invitations? Here at last is Gate 44. A good number, lucky for Poles, absolute magic to us Vilnovites, Belorussolitvins, or Litvino-belorussians.*

The little glassed-in lounge is a transparent box stuffed with a multinational crowd. At the half-open corridor which leads into the plane flight attendants mill about and pilots stride in and out. The time has come to let the people pass into the aerial titan that stands behind the window, powdered with snow like a mammoth of the Arctic. Its beak, or rather nose, looms three stories above the level of the apron. In the hump above the nose where the pilots have their cabin you see movement and the twinkle of little lights, a sign of impending takeoff.

Just then the voice of a German lady comes from a loud-speaker, announcing a delay in starting due to technical diffi-culties. The crowd greets the news with a hostile mutter. They feel caged, just as in wartime before a bombing raid or after evacuation of a threatened city. People even sit on the floor, children cry, the handicapped propel themselves hither and thither in their electric vehicles.

What to do? Why, I know something to do—something just in case, for an hour of need. I can phone Lusia and Marek, friends of mine whom fate has swept all the way here to the Frankfurt area, to one of those little towns like a freshly built movie set where they will film a musical comedy about Bavarian life.

I look for the proper coins, then struggle with a pay phone that is too sophisticated for me.

"Where are you calling from?" (It is she.)

"From right here. From Frankfurt."

"You are at the airport?"

"Yes. Takeoff is delayed."

"And where are you flying to?"

"Australia."

---

* In his verse drama, *Forefathers' Eve*, Adam Mickiewicz prophesied a savior for Poland whom he designated by the cabalistic cipher 44, an equivalent of the Hebrew letters DM. [Trans.]

A moment of silence.

"Not faring too badly, you people."

"I am faring. Just so-so, though. Hitting a snag right at the start."

"Maybe I could manage to meet you there."

"No, no. It's past departure time. Any time now they'll start boarding."

"Why didn't you phone from Warsaw that you were coming through?"

"Things just didn't work out."

"You are forgetting your friends."

"No way! I am always thinking of you all."

"Yeah, that's what they all say. What's new with you?"

"Same old thing."

"And the kids? The cat?"

"Getting on all right. We haven't heard from you in quite a while."

"How come! I sent you a card two weeks ago!"

"But it hasn't come yet."

"Last summer we were on the Easter Islands."

"Easter is when you go to the Easter Islands."

Lusia laughs with alacrity. "It's a pity you are just passing through. When will you plan to come for a little longer? Marek has built a pool in the yard, under a plastic tent. He has to swim a lot because of his back."

"We, too, have our little health gripes."

"Oh! What sort?"

"Nothing sensational. Age, our years. Everything is going to pot, wears out. Even the cat Ivan has aged. Hold on, they are announcing something on the P.A. Bye-bye, then, I'll give you a buzz on my way back."

"Wait, don't hang up . . ."

But all in a flutter, I have pushed the receiver into a hole in the wall of the machine. I have had enough talking, I don't feel up to making conversation. Here is the waiting room again, stuffed with people like a village church and sounding off with another reproving rumble. Takeoff has been postponed again.

But through the window, in this frame of wintry landscape,

a better likeness of me

this German-Polish icon of tentative winter, I see three characters in gray overalls, lugging a stepladder, shuffle and slither
along the icy apron toward our jet plane. The curly black heads
and luxuriant whiskers mark them as *Gastarbeiter*, foreign contract workers. Forebodings immediately clutch my throat, my
spleen, my hernia. Well, I exaggerate a little about the hernia.

So, moseying up to our transcontinental colossus, that godly
chariot, that cosmic rocket, come three exotics who set up their
stepladder (how would one take out that power plant through
whose cowling a ten-ton truck could easily pass); one of them
clambers up to this engine the size of a Warsaw apartment house,
opens some lid, and starts fumbling in the innards of this most
advanced machinery in the solar system with a 16-inch monkey
wrench. Something doesn't work out, though, so he calls down
to his freezing buddies. One of them climbs up onto a rung and
hands the foreman a screwdriver, the exact thing I use at home
to open a can of condensed milk.

At this point, airport staff wheel into our crowded dry aquar ium of a lounge little trolleys loaded with drinks and enormous open sandwiches. This turns our attention away from those three Turks or Greeks, or perhaps Lebanese, who, shivering with cold and evidently without faith in the outcome, fiddle in a Boeing 747 engine with a screwdriver.

We are airborne. In the same ship that was operated on by the *Gastarbeiter*. I am sitting in the nonsmokers' section. In an aisle seat facing a partition. My neighbor is a pretty young lady called Ingrid. I have already found out that she is an actress. I may even have seen her in some film. I also know that she is a fighter for peace or against apartheid, who knows if not for a clean environment, too. From time to time friends come up to her, fellow fighters, and most certainly subscribers to her beauty, talent, and ideology, and hand her various brochures, Xeroxes, documents. She issues fitful orders and instructions. She doesn't take any notice of me, although we have exchanged muttered excuse me's and certainly's.

The plane soars through space like a flying cathedral. It flies serenely, majestically, over mountains covered with golden-white rime, over valleys sunken in dense bluish snow. You feel like nothing so much as jumping with skis through a porthole and zooming schuss down those virgin snowfields.

But it is an illusion. That Antarctica below me, never touched by human foot, is only clouds we are flying over in a space of royal blue, now gradually turning navy.

Earlier, we had been climbing slowly up to our course under the heavens, and the aisles had been steep. All those young mothers who are always on their way somewhere with their children made their way back to their seats braking with their feet against the force of gravity. But outside the window it is slowly turning dark. It means that morning is unhurriedly turning into dusk, for we are flying against the hour, against the sun, along with the rotation of our mother earth.

That Ingrid, the girl seemingly from another planet, looked at me a few times absently, like a person counting up large figures in her head. And she does look as if she had come from another planet, for she is dressed in everything that is most fashionable and least practical. Not to mention her makeup, which would have amazed even Red Indians on their way to the warpath.

But she really stopped reading, counting, and abstractedly scratching her multicolored hair with her ballpoint pen when a stewardess came up and said to me, yes, to me, that the captain was inviting me to the pilots' cabin. She said this in English, although she knew that I don't know English—which had come out when drinks were served at the very beginning. So she informed me in the language of Shakespeare of the whim of Captain Henry S. Landsberg, who had introduced himself to us over the loudspeaker just before takeoff and had later filed past down the right-hand aisle from nose to tail and back, accosting children, sweet-talking old ladies—the good host, our confidence-inspiring leader and protector.

And now he has asked me, a nobody from Poland, to be his guest. Everybody gaped at me, eyes wide open; even some black American colonel. But his human rights didn't have to be fought for by my neighbor, Ingrid, whom I have begun to call Ingryda in my mind for convenience. For this black colonel's chest is all beribboned with medals.

As I said, everybody gaped at me. I wouldn't say with jealousy or envy, but certainly with distinct curiosity. They visually fingered my suit, which was of near-export quality but dated back to Gierek's regime, hence these days could not dazzle those Germans, Japanese, or Belgians. I have long overcome complexes of this sort, and for that matter, I hadn't room for any in my makeup just then. I was completely filled up and loaded down with fear and terror, totally intimidated by being away from home, facing an unknown country, strange people, the onslaught of dreadful diseases, and not least, my ignorance of the English language, that awful handicap that has crippled me all my life. I am always studying and studying English; and the more I do, the better my Russian becomes.

So here I am on my way to the pilots' cabin, seen off by the varicolored eyes of three hundred fifty passengers.

"How do you like the flight?" asks a stewardess.

"Pretty nice. I am glad you speak Polish; and very well, what's more."

"I left the country only ten years ago. My parents did, that is."
"And where do you all live now?"
"In Adelaide. You won't believe this, but the name of my grandmother on my mother's side was Adelajda."

Did I really ever want to see the Southern Cross? What is the Southern Cross to me, assuming there is such a thing? In one of my books I mentioned that constellation two or three times. Somebody at some point must have mesmerized someone with this star cluster, and some third person heaved a helpless sigh at the revelation. The Southern Cross. Orion. The Great Bear. Literature up one side and down another. Metaphorics for the blind. Poetry for the deaf. Literary automatism. Age-long habituation.

Staszek Dygat, after all, also mined this sentimental geography or perhaps astronomy. The Isle of Capri. The Tomb of Kościuszko. The Munich Central Train Station. I followed Staszek with those stars. I sometimes walk in my friend's footsteps, follow his literary trail to remember him by, although his narrative imponderables are a little strange to me. Still, I wend after him, sometimes letting my pen loose to sound like him; let my golden or gold-plated nib vibrate with his melody, that strange half-banal, half-magical lilt.

What is that alien, foreign, unnatural Southern Cross to me? In a dozen hours or so corks will blow out of champagne bottles, and glass in hand, we'll glide or fly under the stratosphere's belly across this imaginary line, never actually drawn on the waist of the globe, that we call the Equator. The stewardesses will put on festive smiles, even the flight crew may emerge, doing up the gold buttons of their uniforms. They will make believe that there is something great about crossing the Equator on board the never-failing Qantas airline.

A bit later the stewardess from Warsaw or Szczebrzeszyn will lean over me and say: "Look through the window. Right there is the Southern Cross."

We stepped into the pilots' cabin, where hundreds of little colored lights winked but otherwise a tight blackness reigned.

Captain Henry S. Landsberg sat at the controls in a snow-white tunic, drinking coffee.

"Here, Tadek, would you like to fly the plane awhile? So you'll have something to tell them about back in Poland?"

"No, I shouldn't. I have bad luck. I might cause a crash."

"The ship is on automatic pilot now. It'll correct you all by itself."

He turned down a kind of jump seat, and I sat on a black stool among the pilots' armchairs; sticking out before me were various lever grips, evidently accelerators for stepping up revolutions, but of what? There they were, those black handles, simply begging the sitter to pull them up or push them down and watch the result.

"I am so glad we are having this flight together. I never believed you when you told me you were flying jumbo jets."

"Now you believe me?"

"Yep."

For this, if you please, was Heniek Landsberg from Wilno. The Laskowskis had found him at some point, *my* Laskowskis from *The Last Day of Summer*, found him or ran into him in Łódź, at the freightyard or the Kalisz Station, as a teenager, in tears or not in tears, but lost, all alone, homeless, and without anyone in charge or taking care of him. So they took him in like a brother, a younger brother who had long been traveling on a repatriation train and finally made it home. This was in 1947.

So Heniek stayed with the Laskowskis, and Mother Olimpiada took care of him like her own; but one day he left and didn't come back. That is, he did return, but only after twenty-some years, about 6 feet 6 inches tall, and in a black pilot's uniform with gold buttons.

And now I am here, looking at the tawny head of Heniek, who is hauling me to Australia, to Sydney or maybe Melbourne, I can't think which just at the moment. He is hauling me just as he used to pull my sled in the Wilno Colony, but I know that he has to undergo hundreds of tests in the course of a year, that he is always adding to his training at courses here and there all over the world, always perfecting himself, practicing, learning, in order to haul rich and poor, bright and dumb, liberal and diehards, all and sundry omnivorous creatures from Europe to the Antipodes. The Antipodes, as they say on travel posters and sports programs.

"Heniek," I pipe up all of a sudden, and don't know how to go on.

He turns his gingery head toward me. "What, Tadek, what is it? Would you like a rest, to lie down for an hour?"

"No, thanks. I'd rather sit here and watch, take in and memorize everything. Isn't it strange that we are flying to the Antipodes together? From Wilno to the kangaroos. Think how this would have amazed our granddads, aunties, uncles, classmates, teachers."

Captain Henry S. Landsberg says something to his colleagues in English. I don't understand what he is saying, for I stayed with the Laskowskis. I never left and never returned.

I look through the pane at the motionless darkness ahead. I see the aquamarine horizon, I make out some timid stars above and around us, I feel the black air about the ship's nose and suddenly sense clearly that we are not flying anywhere, that we are motionless in one place, and beneath us, deep in the earth, elements roar, universes of moderate size arise and perish, good is born and dies in the talons of evil, while what reaches us is only the fine vibration that fills watches, plates, rooms, and our startled brains.

I am returning to my nonsmokers' section. I sit down beside Ingryda, and she looks at me the way girls sometimes looked at me years ago. At irregular intervals the airliner gives a shudder, as if in taking a curve it had hit a roadside post with its overlong tail.

I lean back into the soft armchair and shamelessly inspect the stalwart actress who is flying to Australia to make peace between whites and blacks. Perhaps we shall be staying in the same hotel. Perhaps I will ask her, or she me, to have a drink. But my season is over. It isn't worth it anymore to get together for a drink and then initiate the subtle game of erotic pursuit—the tactics of approach, encirclement, and siege—plotting for the prize of a young woman of mystery. As if there were any mystery women left on earth, as if they hadn't died with Staszek Dygat or even earlier, in the hurricane of war, or later, with the vanishing of horse cabs, little faubourg cafés, and countrywomen selling great bouquets of white jasmine on street corners at night.

I gaze at that girl, Scandinavian or Anglo-American, a little wistfully, for she is paling, fading, as it were, into the grayness of this airplane of dubious reality, while the growl of the engines which those Turks had poked about in with screwdrivers also becomes quieter and more remote. From somewhere in the distance comes the gay jingle of a bell hung from the shaft yoke of a little horse, shaggy with rime, briskly pulling a sleigh along a well-beaten track through stands of thin forest awash in a tremendous flood of moonlight.

Actually, that entire trip to Australia is just something I thought up. For why would I travel there across half the world? Who would be interested in transporting my elderly person from the center of Europe to those Antipodes? Antipodes, antipeoples, antifeelings.

So early in the fall I impudently invented that expedition, a round trip which is undertaken daily by several thousand people. On business or without business. For a wedding or a funeral. Out of boredom or despair.

But this scrap of a journey begun but not completed will be good for something nevertheless.* Nothing is ever quite wasted. Here is evidence, virtually scientific proof, of the form which our great-grandchildren's space travel will take. The speed of light, those hundreds of thousands of miles per second, will be left at the starting line. I propose to you and all of future mankind intergalactic travel by the medium of the imagination. Nothing so swift as human thought, as popular twaddle used to have it.

In our thoughts we shall eventually discover the universe and

---

* As a perverse fate would have it, the following year I did go to Australia; but that is another story.

May Our Lady of Ostra Brama
watch over us

Staś

knock against its black walls. Better to invest in brains than in those hopeless, comic rockets. The mind is the cheapest and most rapid means of locomotion. Our thought and that of our heirs will also unlock the universe of the It or He that governs the universe or is its inspiration.

My most distant journey is a stroll to the Powązki cemetery or the beloved Wolka Węglowa, which puts you in mind of a major sewer construction or a cable-laying line through wasteland. This vast bare graveyard of Warsaw is a landscape of horrible caverns, barely covered with muddy planks and mounds of dried clay and defunct fir wreaths brown with age. I love this cemetery, which so resembles our life—grubby, on the empty side, and terribly sad.

So long, worms. See you in the next world.